100 Recipes from the Kitchen of Mrs. Fields

Time-Life Books
is a division of Time Life Inc.,
a wholly owned subsidiary of
THE TIME INC. BOOK COMPANY

PRESIDENT: John M. Fahey

TIME-LIFE BOOKS

PRESIDENT: Mary Davis

PUBLISHER: Robert H. Smith

**VICE-PRESIDENT AND ASSOCIATE
PUBLISHER:** Susan J. Maruyama

Marketing Director:
Frances C. Mangan

Production Manager:
Prudence G. Harris

Editorial Director:
Blaine Marshall

Senior Art Director:
Robert K. Herndon

Editorial Administrator:
Myrna Traylor-Herndon

Assistant Editor, Research:
Susan Sonnesyn Brooks

Photographer:
Renée Comet

Food Stylist:
Lisa Cherkasky

Second printing 1992. Printed in U.S.A. Published simultaneously in Canada.

TIME-LIFE is a trademark of Time Warner Inc. U.S.A.

Library of Congress Cataloging-in-Publication Data
Fields, Debbi
   Mrs. Fields Cookie Book : one hundred recipes from the kitchen of Mrs. Fields / by Debbi Fields and the editors of Time-Life Books.
         p.   cm.
   Includes index.
   ISBN 0-8094-6712-7 : $17.95 — ISBN 0-8094-6713-5 ; $12.95
   1. Cookies. 2. Desserts. I. Time-Life Books. II. Title.
TX772.F54 1992   641.8'654—dc20   92-9842 CIP

Mrs. Fields® Cookie Book

100 Recipes from the Kitchen of Mrs. Fields

by Debbi Fields
and the Editors of Time-Life Books

TIME
LIFE
CUSTOM
PUBLISHING

Time-Life Books Inc., Alexandria, Virginia

Contents

Randy and Debbi Fields with their daughters (left to right) Ashley, Jennifer, Jenessa, Jessica and McKenzie.

Introduction

I am delighted to present the *Mrs. Fields Cookie Book*—with 100 of my lovingly collected, kitchen-tested, easy-to-follow cookie and dessert recipes.

This is a cookbook created for those of you who bake only occasionally, as well as for the avid bakers among you. My goal has been to create recipes for desserts that look and taste great, and don't take a lot of time and fuss. Besides a cookie for every taste, from Blue-Ribbon Chocolate Chip to Butterscotch Pecan, from classic Oatmeal Raisin to Glazed Almond Crunch, you will also find bars, brownies, pies, cakes, puffs, and other irresistables. This is truly a cookie book-plus!

This book is the product of my lifelong love of baking—and eating—cookies. Baking for others has always been a personal pleasure in my life, starting with making chocolate chip cookies for my family back in Oakland when I was 13. Later I tried out new flavor combinations and tested them on my husband, Randy, and his business colleagues. In 1977 we decided to open our first Mrs. Fields cookie store in Palo Alto. Today, with the help of many wonderful people, my special hobby has grown into an international business that I love, with hundreds of stores worldwide.

Mixing and baking at home is still a favorite family activity. I share the fun with my five daughters as helpers and recipe tasters. After I have measured the ingredients, Ashley and Jennifer eagerly volunteer to break the eggs, help mix, and then shape and drop the dough onto baking sheets, or work the cookie cutters. Their older sisters, Jenessa and Jessica, can make Kids Bake 'Em Cookies and other favorites all by themselves. The girls are masters at decorating sugar cookies for the holidays. Little McKenzie, just teething, plays nearby and, of course, loves to chew on little cookie bits as we go.

My girls made the final selections for this book. If they did not love a recipe, we did not include it. They also helped create new recipes: The Marshmallow Clouds came from Jessica's idea to wrap chocolate dough around a marshmallow and then bake it. We call them "Clouds" because they are heavenly! Like your own family favorites, each one of these recipes has a memory associated with it.

The recipes we present here have been adapted specifically for the home kitchen, using ingredients you have on hand. They are for you to make with and for those you love. These recipes are different from those we bake for our Mrs. Fields Cookie Store customers. Our stores bake with special ingredients made especially for Mrs. Fields and use convection ovens and other professional equipment. The result is a different product than the homebaked version from your own kitchen.

When I am at home with my daughters, we love the variety these recipes offer. Creating and collecting them for this book was a fun, sharing time with our family and friends. I would ask them what would taste yummy together. Then, as I walked down the aisles of supermarkets thinking of new combinations, I would wonder, how about lemon and poppy seed? Brownies with a caramel filling? Coffee, toffee and chocolate? I tried this and changed that. I let my imagination go. One day I went into my pantry, saw malted milk on the shelf, and combined it with some other ingredients I had on hand to create the Malted Milk Cookies. Part of the fun has been developing new combinations and experimenting with new ways of baking. The other day I made a cookie in a waffle iron—it's crispy, cakey and delicious!

What's my secret for making simple recipes that taste great? First I start with the best ingredients available—real butter, real vanilla, real chocolate chips, nothing artificial or imitation. Then I mix the ingredients together—simply, with no unnecessary steps or fussy details. All of these recipes can be made with margarine, but butter makes a difference you can really taste. I do not recommend using shortening, as it does not produce the type of product you expect from Mrs. Fields.

I have included lots of chocolate recipes, because there is nothing quite as tempting to me as biting into a deliciously mouth-watering chocolate cookie. I like to say that some people take flour and add chocolate chips, but Mrs. Fields takes chocolate chips and adds flour!

I have worked to find the right ingredients and measurements to achieve the perfect texture and flavor, so do follow the recipes carefully, and measure properly. Each ingredient listed helps produce the perfect product. Optional ingredients are listed as such. For those of you who live at high altitudes, always reduce by half the given amount of baking soda or powder.

Another thing to keep an eye on is oven temperature. If your cookies are turning dark brown on the bottom when the tops are barely golden, your oven may be too hot. If you can, spend a few dollars on an inexpensive oven thermometer so that you can verify that 300 degrees is really 300 degrees. You don't want your cookies to turn out crispy when they're supposed to be chewy.

I use the "touch" method to know when my cookies are finished baking. When you open your oven door and pull out the baking sheet, touch the cookie lightly. If it sinks, it's obviously underbaked. If it's hard as a rock, you've overbaked it. But if the cookie has spring to it and you can move it a bit, the cookie is perfect.

Many of the recipes say, "Transfer cookies to a cool, flat surface" after baking. This simply means take a spatula and move the cookies from the hot baking sheet directly onto your countertop or a cool baking sheet so they won't continue to bake. I don't bother with paper towels or racks. Do be careful not to put the cookies on a chopping board, or you may pick up the garlic or onion you chopped for last night's dinner!

My recipes include cookies of various shapes and sizes to suit different occasions. Large cookies—such as the Soft and Chewy Peanut Butter—are great for keeping in the cookie jar for those times when you or your kids need a snack in a hurry. (To save time and get a nice rounded shape, try scooping the dough with an ice-cream scoop.) Other recipes make delicate cookies for more formal occasions—the Linzer, the Chocolate-Glazed Shortbread, or the Brown Buttercrunch—any of which could be served at an afternoon luncheon or meeting. Brownies or bar cookies are perfect for making ahead and freezing, for taking to a picnic, or for packing in your children's lunch boxes. For added nutrition, some recipes include natural sweeteners, such as carrots, pineapple or apricot nectar.

I hope you will enjoy making and sharing these recipes with those you love. Recipes made from the heart are sure to be delicious. And when you bake, by all means include your family—every age can help out in some way.

So many people have helped with this book—testing, tasting, helping me create the recipes. On weekends my kitchen has been filled with friends and family. We all hope the *Mrs. Fields Cookie Book* will become a favorite source whenever you or your family is in the mood for, say, Super Fudge Brownies, Mocha Mousse Cheesecake, or perhaps a Macadamia Nut Surprise. Ready to have fun?

Drop Cookies

2½ cups all-purpose flour
½ tsp. baking soda
¼ tsp. salt
1 cup dark brown sugar, firmly packed
½ cup white sugar
1 cup salted butter, softened
2 large eggs
2 tsp. pure vanilla extract
2 cups (12 oz.) semisweet chocolate chips

Yield: 3½ dozen

Preheat oven to 300° F.

In medium bowl combine flour, soda and salt. Mix well with wire whisk. Set aside.

In a large bowl with an electric mixer blend sugars at medium speed. Add butter and mix to form a grainy paste, scraping down the sides of the bowl. Add eggs and vanilla extract, and mix at medium speed until just blended. Do not overmix.

Add the flour mixture and chocolate chips, and blend at low speed until just mixed. Do not overmix.

Drop by rounded tablespoons onto an ungreased cookie sheet, 2 inches apart. Bake 22-24 minutes or until golden brown. Transfer cookies immediately to a cool surface with a spatula.

Drop each heaping tablespoon of dough onto the cookie sheet, taking care to leave about 2 inches between each cookie. As they bake, the cookies will spread quite a bit.

Creamy Lemon Macadamia Cookies

Preheat oven to 300° F.

In a medium bowl combine flour, soda and salt. Mix well with wire whisk and set aside.

In a large bowl blend sugars well with an electric mixer set at medium speed. Add the butter and cream cheese, and mix to form a smooth paste. Add the egg and lemon extract, and beat at medium speed until light and soft. Scrape down sides of bowl occasionally.

Add the flour mixture and macadamia nuts. Blend at low speed just until combined. Do not overmix.

Drop by rounded tablespoons onto ungreased cookie sheets, 2 inches apart. Bake 23-25 minutes. Immediately transfer cookies with a spatula to a cool flat surface.

2 cups all-purpose flour
½ tsp. baking soda
¼ tsp. salt
1 cup light brown sugar, packed
½ cup white sugar
½ cup salted butter, softened
4 oz. cream cheese, softened
1 large egg
2 tsp. pure lemon extract
1½ cups (7 oz.) whole macadamia nuts, unsalted

Yield: 3 dozen

Soft and Chewy Peanut Butter Cookies

2 cups all-purpose flour
½ tsp. baking soda
¼ tsp. salt
1¼ cups dark brown sugar, firmly packed
1¼ cups white sugar
1 cup salted butter, softened
3 large eggs
1 cup creamy peanut butter
2 tsp. pure vanilla extract

Yield: 3½ dozen

Preheat oven to 300° F.

In a medium bowl combine flour, soda and salt. Mix well with a wire whisk. Set aside.

In a large bowl blend sugars using an electric mixer set at medium speed. Add butter and mix to form a grainy paste, scraping the sides of the bowl. Add eggs, peanut butter and vanilla, and mix at medium speed until light and fluffy.

Add the flour mixture and mix at low speed until just mixed. Do not overmix.

Drop by rounded tablespoons onto an ungreased cookie sheet, 1½ inches apart. With a wet fork gently press a crisscross pattern on top of cookies. Bake for 18-22 minutes until cookies are slightly brown along edges. Transfer cookies immediately to cool surface with a spatula.

As a variation, add 2 cups coarsely chopped semisweet chocolate bar or 2 cups semisweet chocolate chips to the flour mixture, then bake as directed.

After the dough is dropped onto the cookie sheets, use a fork to press a crisscross pattern in each cookie. In order to keep dough from sticking to the fork as you proceed, dip the fork in water after each cookie is flattened.

Oatmeal Raisin Chews

Preheat oven to 300° F.

In a medium bowl combine flour, soda, salt and oats. Mix well with wire whisk and set aside.

In a large bowl blend sugars with electric mixer set at medium speed. Add butter and mix to form a grainy paste. Scrape down sides of bowl, then add honey, vanilla and eggs. Mix at medium speed until light and fluffy.

Add the flour mixture, raisins and walnuts, and blend at low speed just until combined. Do not overmix.

Drop by rounded tablespoons onto ungreased cookie sheets, 1½ inches apart. Bake for 22-24 minutes or until cookies are light golden brown. Immediately transfer cookies with a spatula to a cool flat surface.

2¼ cups all-purpose flour
½ tsp. baking soda
¼ tsp. salt
1 cup quick oats (not instant)
1 cup dark brown sugar, packed
½ cup white sugar
1 cup salted butter, softened
2 Tbsp. honey
2 tsp. pure vanilla extract
2 large eggs
1½ cups (8 oz.) raisins
½ cup (3 oz.) walnuts, chopped
(optional)

Yield: 3 dozen without walnuts
3½ dozen with walnuts

Pumpkin Spice Cookies

2½ cups all-purpose flour
½ tsp. baking soda
¼ tsp. salt
2 tsp. pumpkin pie spice
1 cup dark brown sugar, packed
½ cup white sugar
¾ cup salted butter, softened
1 large egg
1 cup pumpkin
(canned or freshly cooked)
1 tsp. pure vanilla extract
1 cup (6 oz.) raisins
½ cup (2 oz.) walnuts, chopped

Yield: 3 dozen

Preheat oven to 300° F.

In a medium bowl combine flour, soda, salt and pumpkin pie spice. Mix well with a wire whisk and set aside.

In a large bowl blend sugars with an electric mixer set at medium speed. Add the butter and beat to form a grainy paste. Scrape sides of bowl, then add egg, pumpkin and vanilla. Beat at medium speed until light and fluffy.

Add the flour mixture, raisins and walnuts. Blend at low speed just until combined. Do not overmix.

Drop by rounded tablespoons onto ungreased cookie sheets, 1½ inches apart. Bake 22-24 minutes until cookies are slightly brown along edges. Immediately transfer cookies with a spatula to a cool surface.

Chocolate Raisin Cookies

Preheat oven to 300° F.

In a double-boiler over hot but not boiling water, melt ½ cup butter and the unsweetened chocolate. Remove from heat. Set aside.

In medium bowl combine flour, soda and salt. Mix well with a wire whisk. Set aside.

In large bowl with an electric mixer blend sugars at medium speed until fluffy. Add the remaining ½ cup butter and mix to form a grainy paste, scraping down the sides of the bowl. Add eggs and vanilla, and beat at medium speed until light and fluffy. Add melted chocolate and blend until thoroughly combined.

Add the flour mixture, raisins and chocolate chips. Blend at low speed until just combined. Do not overmix.

Drop by rounded tablespoons onto ungreased baking sheets, 2 inches apart. Bake for 20-22 minutes or until set. Transfer to cool, flat surface immediately with a spatula.

1 cup salted butter, divided
2 oz. unsweetened baking chocolate
2¼ cups all-purpose flour
½ tsp. baking soda
¼ tsp. salt
1 cup dark brown sugar, firmly packed
½ cup white sugar
2 large eggs
2 tsp. pure vanilla extract
1½ cups (9 oz.) raisins
1 cup (6 oz.) semisweet chocolate chips

Yield: 4 dozen

Cookies:
2½ cups all-purpose flour
½ tsp. baking soda
¼ tsp. salt
1½ cups dark brown sugar, firmly packed
1 cup salted butter, softened
2 large eggs
2 tsp. pure vanilla extract*
1 cup (4 oz.) chopped pecans
1 cup (3 oz.) whole pecans

Caramel Glaze:
8 oz. caramels
¼ cup heavy cream

Yield: 2½ dozen

*For an authentic butterscotch flavor, the vanilla may be substituted with an equal quantity of scotch whiskey.

Preheat oven to 300° F.

In medium bowl combine flour, soda and salt. Mix well with a wire whisk. Set aside.

In large bowl with electric mixer beat sugar and butter. Mix to form a grainy paste, scraping down the sides of the bowl. Add eggs and vanilla, and beat at medium speed until soft and lumpy. Add the flour mixture and chopped pecans, and mix at low speed until just combined. Do not overmix.

Drop dough by rounded tablespoons 2 inches apart onto ungreased cookie sheets. Place one whole pecan in center of each cookie. Bake 23-25 minutes or until cookie edges begin to brown lightly. Transfer immediately to cool, flat surface with a spatula.

To prepare the caramel glaze: Melt the caramels with the cream in a small saucepan over low heat. Stir with a wooden spoon until smooth. Remove from heat.

Drizzle cooled cookies with caramel glaze into desired pattern using a spoon or fork.

Drizzle cookies with the caramel glaze for an extra touch of creamy flavor. Make sure that the glaze flows from the fork in a thin stream in order to achieve the most decorative effect.

Lemon Poppy Seed Cookies

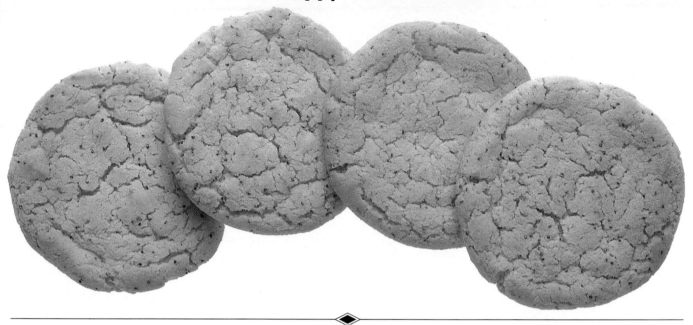

Preheat oven 300° F.

In a medium bowl combine flour, baking soda, lemon zest, coriander and poppyseeds. Mix well with a wire whisk and set aside.

In a large bowl cream butter and sugar with electric mixer at medium speed until mixture forms a grainy paste. Scrape down sides of bowl, then add yolks, egg and lemon extract. Beat at medium speed until light and fluffy.

Add the flour mixture and mix at low speed just until combined. Do not overmix.

Drop by rounded tablespoons onto ungreased cookie sheets, 2 inches apart. Bake for 23-25 minutes until cookies are slightly brown along edges. Immediately transfer cookies with a spatula to a cool surface.

2 cups all-purpose flour
½ tsp. baking soda
1½ tsp. freshly grated lemon zest
1 tsp. ground coriander
2 Tbsp. poppy seeds
¾ cup salted butter, softened
1 cup white sugar
2 large egg yolks
1 large whole egg
1½ tsp. pure lemon extract

Yield: 2 dozen

Scraping down the sides of the bowl with a rubber spatula after beating (far left) ensures that the butter and sugar are thoroughly blended to provide a consistent base for the remaining ingredients. Additional beating (left) puts air into the batter, yielding a light and crunchy cookie.

Malted Milk Cookies

2½ cups all-purpose flour
¾ cup plain malted milk powder
½ tsp. baking soda
¼ tsp. salt
1 cup white sugar
½ cup light brown sugar, firmly packed
1 cup salted butter, softened
2 large eggs
2 tsp. pure vanilla extract
2 Tbsp. sweetened condensed milk
2 cups (12 oz.) milk chocolate chips

Yield: 3½ dozen

Preheat oven to 300° F.

In medium bowl combine flour, malted milk powder, soda and salt. Mix well with a wire whisk. Set aside.

Blend sugars in a large bowl using an electric mixer set at medium speed. Add butter and mix, occasionally scraping down the sides of the bowl. Add the eggs, vanilla and condensed milk, and beat at medium speed until light and fluffy.

Add the flour mixture and chocolate chips, and blend at low speed until just combined. Do not overmix.

Drop by rounded tablespoons onto ungreased cookie sheets, 2 inches apart. Bake 24-25 minutes until cookies are slightly brown along edges. Transfer cookies immediately to cool surface with a spatula.

Carrot Fruit Jumbles

Preheat oven to 350°F.

In a medium bowl combine flour, soda, baking powder, cloves, cinnamon, salt and oats. Mix well with a wire whisk and set aside.

In a large bowl with an electric mixer, blend sugars. Add butter and mix to form a grainy paste. Scrape down sides of bowl.

Add eggs and vanilla, and beat at medium speed until light and fluffy. Add carrots, pineapple and nuts, and blend until combined. Batter will appear lumpy.

Add flour mixture and blend at low speed until just combined. Do not overmix.

Drop by rounded teaspoons onto ungreased baking sheets, 1½ inches apart. Bake 13-15 minutes, taking care not to brown cookies. Immediately transfer cookies with a spatula to a cool, flat surface.

2½ cups all purpose flour
1 tsp. baking soda
½ tsp. baking powder
½ tsp. ground cloves
2 tsp. ground cinnamon
¼ tsp. salt
1 cup quick oats (not instant)
¾ cup dark brown sugar, packed
¾ cup white sugar
1 cup salted butter, softened
2 large eggs
2 tsp. pure vanilla extract
2 cups grated carrot
(2 or 3 medium carrots)
½ cup crushed pineapple, drained
1 cup (4 oz.) chopped walnuts

Yield: 4 dozen

1¼ cups all-purpose flour
½ tsp. baking soda
⅛ tsp. salt
½ cup salted butter, softened
¼ cup white sugar
½ cup honey
1 cup (6 oz) semisweet chocolate chips

Yield: 2 dozen

Preheat oven 300° F.

In a smal bowl combine flour, soda and salt. Mix well with a wire whisk and set aside.

In another medium bowl blend butter, sugar and honey with an electric mixer at medium speed. Beat until light and soft, then scrape sides of bowl.

Add the flour mixture and chocolate chips, and blend at low speed just until combined. Do not overmix.

Drop dough by rounded teaspoonfuls onto ungreased cookie sheets, 1½ inches apart. Bake 18-20 minutes or until light golden brown. Immediately transfer cookies with a spatula to a cool, flat surface.

Pecan Supremes

Preheat oven to 300° F.

In a medium bowl combine flour, soda, salt and oats. Mix well with wire whisk and set aside.

In a large bowl blend sugars with an electric mixer at medium speed. Add butter and mix to form a grainy paste. Scrape down sides of bowl, then add eggs and vanilla. Beat at medium speed until light and fluffy.

Add the flour mixture, pecans and chocolate chips, and blend at low speed just until combined. Do not overmix.

Drop dough by rounded tablespoons onto ungreased cookie sheets, 1½ inches apart. Bake for 20-22 minutes. Immediately transfer cookies with a spatula to a cool, flat surface.

2 cups all-purpose flour
½ tsp. baking soda
¼ tsp. salt
¾ cup quick oats
¾ cup dark brown sugar, packed
¾ cup white sugar
1 cup salted butter, softened
2 large eggs
2 tsp. pure vanilla extract
1 cup (4 oz.) chopped pecans
1 cup (6 oz.) semisweet chocolate chips

Yield: 3 dozen

Mocha Chunk Cookies

2½ cups all-purpose flour
⅓ cup unsweetened cocoa powder
½ tsp. baking soda
¼ tsp. salt
2 tsp. instant coffee crystals
(French roast or other dark coffee)
2 tsp. coffee liqueur
1 cup white sugar
¾ cup dark brown sugar, packed
1 cup salted butter, softened
2 large eggs
2 cups (10 oz.) semisweet chocolate
bar, coarsely chopped

Yield: 4 dozen

Preheat oven 300° F.

In a medium bowl combine flour, cocoa, soda and salt. Mix well with a wire whisk and set aside.

In a small bowl dissolve coffee crystals in coffee liqueur and set aside.

In a large bowl blend sugars with an electric mixer at medium speed. Add butter and mix to form a grainy paste. Scrape down sides of bowl. Then add eggs and dissolved coffee crystals, and beat at medium speed until smooth.

Add the flour mixture and chocolate chunks, and blend at low speed just until combined. Do not overmix.

Drop by rounded tablespoonfuls onto ungreased cookie sheet, 2 inches apart. Bake for 23-25 minutes. Immediately transfer cookies with a spatula to a cool, flat surface.

Banana Nut Cookies

Preheat oven to 300° F.

In medium bowl combine flour, soda and salt. Mix well with a wire whisk. Set aside.

In large bowl with an electric mixer blend sugars at medium speed. Add butter and mix to form a grainy paste, scraping down the sides of the bowl. Add egg, liqueur and banana, and beat at medium speed until smooth.

Add the flour mixture, 1 cup of the chocolate chips and the walnuts, and blend at low speed until just combined. Do not overmix.

Drop by rounded tablespoons onto ungreased cookie sheets, 2 inches apart. Sprinkle cookies with chocolate chips, 6 to 8 per cookie. Bake 25-27 minutes or until cookie edges begin to brown. Transfer immediately to a cool surface with a spatula.

2⅔ cups all-purpose flour
½ tsp. baking soda
¼ tsp. salt
1 cup light brown sugar, firmly packed
½ cup white sugar
1 cup salted butter, softened
1 large egg
1 tsp. crême de banana liqueur or pure banana extract
¾ cup (1 medium) mashed ripe banana
2 cups (12 oz.) semisweet chocolate chips
1 cup (4 oz.) chopped walnuts

Yield: 4 dozen

Nutty White Chunk Cookies

2¼ cups all-purpose flour
½ tsp. baking soda
¼ tsp. salt
1 cup light brown sugar, firmly packed
½ cup white sugar
¾ cup salted butter, softened
2 large eggs
2 tsp. pure vanilla extract
1 cup (4 oz.) pecans, chopped
1½ cups (8 oz.) white chocolate bar, coarsely chopped

Preheat oven to 300° F.

In medium bowl combine flour, soda and salt. Mix well with a wire whisk. Set aside.

In large bowl with an electric mixer blend sugars at medium speed. Add butter and mix to form a grainy paste, scraping down the sides of the bowl. Add eggs and vanilla, and beat at medium speed until light and fluffy.

Add the flour mixture, pecans and white chocolate, and blend at low speed until just combined. Do not overmix.

Drop by rounded tablespoons onto ungreased cookie sheets, 2 inches apart. Bake 20-22 minutes or until edges just begin to turn golden brown. Use a spatula to transfer cookies immediately to a cool, flat surface.

Pineapple Paradise Cookies

Preheat oven to 300° F.

In medium bowl combine flour and baking soda. Mix well with a wire whisk. Set aside.

In large bowl with an electric mixer blend sugars. Add butter and mix to form a grainy paste, scraping down the sides of the bowl. Add egg, vanilla, crushed pineapple and pineapple juice and beat on medium speed until smooth.

Add the flour mixture and blend at low speed until just combined. Do not overmix.

Drop by rounded tablespoons onto ungreased baking sheets, 2 inches apart. Sprinkle lightly with shredded coconut, if desired.

Bake 22-24 minutes or until cookies begin to turn lightly brown at edges. Transfer immediately to cool flat surface with spatula.

3 cups all-purpose flour
½ tsp. baking soda
¾ cup dark brown sugar, firmly packed
¾ cup white sugar
1 cup salted butter, softened
1 large egg
2 tsp. pure vanilla extract
one 8-ounce can crushed pineapple or 1 cup fresh finely chopped pineapple, well drained
1 Tbsp. pineapple juice
¼ cup sweetened shredded coconut

Yield: 3 dozen

2 cups all-purpose flour
¼ tsp. salt
½ tsp. baking soda
½ cup dark brown sugar, packed
½ cup white sugar
¾ cup salted butter, softened
1 large egg
2 tsp. pure vanilla extract
1 cup crispy rice cereal
1½ cups (8 oz.) crispy rice chocolate
bar, coarsely chopped

Yield: 3 dozen

Preheat oven to 300° F.

In a medium bowl combine flour, salt and soda. Mix well with a wire whisk and set aside.

In a large bowl blend sugars with an electric mixer at medium speed. Add butter and mix to form a grainy paste. Scrape down sides of bowl, then add egg and vanilla. Beat at medium speed until light and fluffy.

Add flour mixture, rice cereal and chocolate chunks. Blend at low speed just until combined. Do not overmix.

Drop by rounded tablespoons onto ungreased cookie sheets, 2 inches apart. Bake for 22-24 minutes. Immediately transfer cookies with a spatula to a cool, flat surface.

Apple Oatmeal Cookies

Preheat oven to 300° F.

In medium bowl combine flour, oats, salt, soda, cinnamon, cloves and lemon zest. Mix well with a wire whisk. Set aside.

Cream sugar and butter together in a large bowl using an electric mixer. Add egg, applesauce and honey and beat at medium speed until smooth.

Add the flour mixture, fresh apple and raisins, and blend at low speed until just combined. Do not overmix. Dough will be quite soft.

Drop by rounded tablespoons onto ungreased baking sheets, 1½ inches apart. If you wish, sprinkle the cookies with oats. Bake 23-25 minutes or until bottoms are golden.

Cookies:
2½ cups all-purpose flour
1 cup quick oats (not instant)
½ tsp. salt
1 tsp. baking soda
1 tsp. ground cinnamon
¼ tsp. ground cloves
2 tsp. grated lemon zest
(1 medium lemon)
1 cup dark brown sugar, firmly packed
¾ cup salted butter, softened
1 large egg
½ cup unsweetened applesauce
½ cup honey
1 cup fresh apple, peeled and finely chopped (1 medium apple)
1 cup (6 oz.) raisins

Topping:
½ cup quick oats

Yield: 4 dozen

2¼ cups all-purpose flour
½ cup unsweetened cocoa powder
½ tsp. baking soda
¼ tsp. salt
1 cup dark brown sugar, firmly packed
¾ cup white sugar
1 cup salted butter, softened
3 large eggs
2 tsp. pure vanilla extract
1 cup (5¼ oz.) semisweet chocolate bar, coarsely chopped
1 cup (5¼ oz.) white chocolate bar, coarsely chopped

Yield: 3 dozen

Preheat oven to 300° F.

In medium bowl combine flour, cocoa, soda and salt. Mix well with a wire whisk. Set aside.

Blend sugars in a large bowl using an electric mixer set at medium speed. Add butter and mix to form a grainy paste, scraping down the sides of the bowl. Add eggs and vanilla, and beat at medium speed until smooth.

Add the flour mixture and chocolates, and blend at low speed until just combined. Do not overmix.

Drop by rounded tablespoons onto ungreased cookie sheets, 2 inches apart. Bake 23-25 minutes. Transfer cookies immediately to a cool, flat surface.

Preheat oven to 300° F.

In medium bowl combine flour, baking powder and salt with wire whisk. Set aside.

Combine sugars in a large bowl using an electric mixer set at medium speed. Add butter and beat until batter is grainy. Add egg, sour cream and vanilla, and beat at medium speed until light and fluffy. Scrape bowl. Add the flour mixture, and blend at low speed until just combined. Do not overmix.

Place chocolate chips in double boiler over hot but not boiling water. Stir constantly until melted. Or, place chips in a microwave-proof bowl and microwave on high, stirring every 20 seconds until melted.

Cool chocolate for a few minutes and pour over cookie batter. Using a wooden spoon or rubber spatula, lightly fold melted chocolate into the dough. Do not mix chocolate completely into cookie dough.

Drop by rounded tablespoons, 2 inches apart, onto ungreased cookie sheets. Bake 23-25 minutes. Do not brown. Quickly transfer cookies to a cool surface.

2 cups all-purpose flour
½ tsp. baking powder
¼ tsp. salt
½ cup light brown sugar, firmly packed
½ cup white sugar
½ cup salted butter, softened
1 large egg
½ cup (4 oz.) sour cream
1 tsp. pure vanilla extract
1 cup (6 oz.) semisweet chocolate chips

Yield: 2½ dozen

Fold the cool melted chocolate into the cookie batter, stirring lightly with a wooden spoon (far left). Continue stirring only until the chocolate is well distributed and creates a swirled, marbled pattern (left).

Chocolate Mint Cookies

2⅔ cups all-purpose flour
½ tsp. baking soda
¼ tsp. salt
½ cup unsweetened cocoa powder
¾ cup light brown sugar, packed
⅔ cup white sugar
1 cup salted butter, softened
3 large eggs
1 tsp. pure mint extract
1¾ cups (10 oz.)
mint chocolate chips

Yield: 3 dozen

Preheat oven to 300° F.

In a medium bowl combine flour, soda, salt and cocoa powder. Mix well with a wire whisk and set aside.

In a large bowl blend sugars with an electric mixer at medium speed. Add butter and beat to form a grainy paste. Scrapes sides of bowl, then add eggs and mint extract. Beat at medium speed until light and fluffy.

Add the flour mixture and chocolate chips, and blend at low speed just until combined. Do not overmix.

Drop dough by rounded tablespoonfuls onto ungreased cookie sheets, 1½ inches apart. Bake for 19-21 minutes. Immediately transfer cookies with a spatula to a cool, flat surface.

Lemon Chocolate Chip Buttons

Preheat oven to 300° F.

In a medium bowl combine flour, soda and coriander with a wire whisk. Set aside.

In a large bowl cream butter and sugar with an electric mixer at medium speed to form a grainy paste. Add eggs and lemon extract, and beat well. Scrape down sides of bowl.

Add the flour mixture and the chocolate chips, and blend at low speed just until combined. Do not overmix.

Drop dough by teaspoonfuls onto ungreased baking sheets, 1½ inches apart. Bake for 14-15 minutes on center rack of oven. Do not brown. Immediately transfer with a spatula to a cool surface.

2 cups all-purpose flour
½ tsp. baking soda
1 tsp. ground coriander
¾ cup salted butter, softened
1 cup white sugar
2 large eggs
1½ tsp. pure lemon extract
1½ cups (9 oz.) miniature chocolate chips

Yield: 4 dozen

Double-Rich Chocolate Cookies

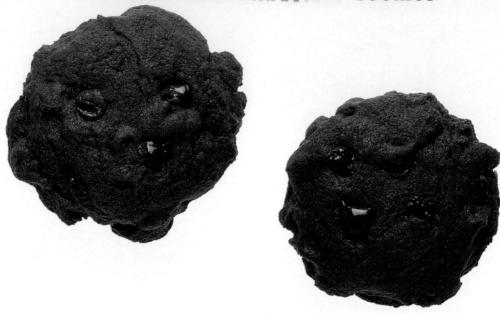

2½ cups all-purpose flour
½ tsp. baking soda
¼ tsp. salt
½ cup unsweetened cocoa powder
1 cup dark brown sugar, packed
¾ cup white sugar
1 cup salted butter, softened
3 large eggs
2 tsp. pure vanilla
2 cups (12 oz.)
semisweet chocolate chips

Yield: 4 dozen

Preheat oven 300° F.

In a medium bowl combine flour, soda, salt and cocoa powder. Mix well with a wire whisk and set aside.

In a large bowl blend sugars with an electric mixer at medium speed. Add butter and beat to form a grainy paste. Scrape down sides of bowl, then add eggs and vanilla. Beat at medium speed until light and fluffy.

Add the flour mixture and chocolate chips, and blend at low speed just until combined. Do not overmix.

Drop dough by rounded tablespoons onto ungreased cookie sheets, 1½ inches apart. Bake for 21-23 minutes. Immediately transfer cookies with a spatula to a cool surface.

Mandarin and Marmalade Cookies

Preheat oven to 300° F.

In a medium bowl combine flour and baking powder. Mix well with a wire whisk and set aside.

In a large bowl blend butter and sugar with an electric mixer to form a grainy paste. Add egg and orange marmalade, and beat at medium speed until smooth. Add the flour mixture and the oranges, and blend at low speed just until combined. Do not overmix.

Drop by rounded tablespoonfuls onto ungreased baking sheets, 1½ inches apart. Bake 24-25 minutes or until the bottoms of cookies begin to brown. Transfer with a spatula to a cool, flat surface.

2¾ cups all-purpose flour
1 tsp. baking powder
1 cup salted butter, softened
1 cup white sugar
1 large egg
½ cup orange marmalade
one 10 oz. can mandarin oranges,
drained and chopped

Yield: 3½ dozen

Orange Chocolate Chunk Cookies

2½ cups all-purpose flour
½ tsp. baking soda
¼ tsp. salt
1 tsp. grated orange peel
(one medium orange)
1 cup white sugar
½ cup light brown sugar, packed
1 cup salted butter, softened
2 large eggs
1 tsp. pure orange extract
1½ cups (8 oz.) semisweet chocolate
bar, coarsely chopped

Preheat oven to 300° F.

In a medium bowl combine flour, soda, salt and orange peel. Mix well with a wire whisk and set aside.

In a large bowl blend sugars with electric mixer at medium speed. Add butter and beat to form a grainy paste, scraping sides of bowl if needed. Add eggs and orange extract, and beat at medium speed until light and fluffy.

Add the flour mixture and chopped chocolate. Blend at low speed just until combined. Do not overmix.

Drop by rounded tablespoons onto ungreased cookie sheets, 1½ inches apart. Bake for 22-24 minutes until cookies are slightly brown along edges. Transfer cookies immediately to a cool surface with a spatula.

Eggnog Cookies

Preheat oven to 300° F.

In a medium bowl combine flour, baking powder, cinnamon and nutmeg. Mix well with a wire whisk and set aside.

In a large bowl cream sugar and butter with an electric mixer to form a grainy paste. Add eggnog, vanilla and egg yolks and beat at medium speed until smooth.

Add the flour mixture and beat at low speed just until combined. Do not overmix.

Drop by rounded teaspoonfuls onto ungreased baking sheets, 1 inch apart. Sprinkle lightly with nutmeg. Bake for 23-25 minutes or until bottoms turn light brown. Transfer to cool, flat surface immediately with a spatula.

2¼ cups all-purpose flour
1 tsp. baking powder
½ tsp. ground cinnamon
½ tsp. ground nutmeg
1¼ cups white sugar
¾ cups salted butter, softened
½ cup eggnog
1 tsp. pure vanilla extract
2 large egg yolks
1 Tbsp. ground nutmeg

Yield: 3 dozen

2 cups all-purpose flour
½ tsp. baking powder
1 cup quick oats (not instant)
1 cup salted butter, softened
1½ cups light brown sugar, packed
¼ cup unsulphured molasses
2 tsp. brandy
2 tsp. pure vanilla extract
2 tsp. almond extract
2 large eggs
½ cup (3 oz.) raisins
1 cup (4 oz.) chopped pecans
½ cup (2 oz.) chopped almonds
2 cups (13.5 oz.) candied cherries,
chopped

Yield: 4½ dozen

Preheat oven to 300° F.

In a medium bowl combine flour, baking powder and oats. Mix well with a wire whisk and set aside.

In a large bowl cream butter and sugar with an electric mixer at medium speed. Mix to form a grainy paste. Add molasses, brandy, almond and vanilla extracts and eggs; beat until smooth.

Add the flour mixture, raisins, pecans, almonds and cherries. Blend at low speed just until combined. Do not overmix.

Drop by rounded tablespoonfuls onto ungreased baking sheets, 1½ inches apart. Bake for 22-24 minutes or until cookies are set.

Let cookies set on pan for a few minutes, then transfer to a cool, flat surface. Top each cookie with a candied cherry half.

These cookies are fruitcake made easy—you just blend everything in your mixer—first the dry ingredients, then the wet, and finally the fruit pieces. A hand mixer or a stand-up mixer both work fine.

Chocolate Chip Raisin Cookies

Preheat oven to 300°F.

In medium bowl combine flour and baking powder. Mix well with wire whisk. Set aside.

Blend sugars in a large bowl using an electric mixer set at medium speed. Add butter and mix until grainy, scraping down the sides of the bowl. Add eggs and vanilla extract, and mix at medium speed until smooth.

Add the flour mixture, raisins and chocolate chips. Blend at low speed until just combined. Do not overmix.

Drop by rounded tablespoons onto ungreased baking sheets, 1½ inches apart. Bake 22-24 minutes. Transfer cookies immediately to a cool, flat surface using a spatula.

2 cups all-purpose flour
½ tsp. baking powder
⅓ cup light brown sugar, firmly packed
1 cup white sugar
1 cup salted butter, softened
2 large eggs
2 tsp. pure vanilla extract
2 cups (12 oz.) raisins
2 cups (12 oz.) semisweet chocolate chips

Yield: 4½ dozen

Apricot Nectar Cookies

2¾ cups all-purpose flour
1 tsp. baking soda
¾ cup white sugar
¼ cup dark brown sugar, packed
1 cup salted butter, softened
1 large egg
¼ cup apricot nectar
½ cup apricot preserves
¾ cup dried apricots, chopped

Yield: 3½ dozen

Preheat oven to 300° F.

In a medium bowl combine flour and baking soda. Mix well with a wire whisk and set aside.

In a large bowl blend sugars with an electric mixer at medium speed. Add butter and mix to form a grainy paste. Scrape down sides of bowl. Then add egg, apricot nectar and apricot preserves; beat at medium speed until smooth.

Add the flour mixture and apricots, and blend on low just until combined. Do not overmix.

Drop by rounded tablespoonfuls onto ungreased baking sheets, 1½ inches apart. Bake 22-24 minutes or until cookies just begin to brown at bottom edges.

Remove from oven and let cookies cool on baking sheet 5 minutes before transferring to a cool flat surface with a spatula.

Cholesterol-Free Chocolate Chip Cookies

Preheat oven to 300° F.

In medium bowl combine flour, soda and salt. Mix well with a wire whisk and set aside.

In large bowl blend sugars with an electric mixer. Add margarine, and mix to form a grainy paste.

In small bowl, beat egg whites until fluffy. Add egg whites, honey and vanilla to sugar mixture, and beat until smooth. Scrape down sides of bowl.

Add the flour mixture and chocolate chips, and blend on low speed just until combined. Do not overmix.

Drop by rounded tablespoonfuls onto ungreased cookie sheets, 1½ inches apart. Bake for 18-20 minutes until lightly browned. Immediately transfer cookies with a spatula to a cool, flat surface.

2½ cups all-purpose flour
½ tsp. baking soda
¼ tsp. salt
¾ cup dark brown sugar, packed
½ cup white sugar
½ cup margarine
3 large egg whites
2 Tbsp. honey
2 tsp. pure vanilla extract
2 cups (12 oz.)
semisweet chocolate chips

Yield: 3½ dozen

Peanut Butter Oatmeal Ranch Cookies

¾ cup whole wheat flour
¾ cup all-purpose flour
½ tsp. baking powder
1 cup oats (old fashioned or quick)
1 cup light brown sugar, packed
½ cup salted butter, softened
½ cup creamy peanut butter
¼ cup honey
2 large eggs
2 tsp. pure vanilla extract
1 cup (6 oz.) raisins
½ cup (3 oz.) sunflower seeds

Yield: 3 dozen

Preheat oven to 300° F.

In a medium bowl combine flours, baking powder and oats. Mix well with a wire whisk and set aside.

In a large bowl beat sugar and butter with an electric mixer at medium speed to form a grainy paste. Blend together the peanut butter, honey, eggs and vanilla. Scrape down sides of bowl.

Add the flour mixture, raisins and sunflower seeds. Blend at low speed just until combined. Do not overmix.

Drop by rounded tablespoonfuls onto ungreased baking sheets, 2 inches apart. Bake for 23-25 minutes until bottoms turn golden brown. Immediately transfer cookies with a spatula to a cool, flat surface.

Cashew and Coconut Cookies

Preheat oven to 300° F.

In a medium bowl combine flour, soda and salt. Mix well with a wire whisk and set aside.

In a medium bowl combine sugars with an electric mixer at medium speed. Add butter and mix to form a grainy paste. Add eggs and vanilla, and beat until smooth.

Add flour mixture, coconut, cashews and dates. Blend at low speed just until combined. Do not overmix.

Drop by rounded tablespoonfuls onto ungreased baking sheets, 2 inches apart. Sprinkle tops lightly with reserved coconut.

Bake for 23-25 minutes or until bottoms turn golden brown. With a spatula, transfer to a cool, flat surface.

2¼ cups all-purpose flour
½ tsp. baking soda
¼ tsp. salt
¾ cup light brown sugar, packed
½ cup white sugar
¾ cup salted butter, softened
2 large eggs
2 tsp. pure vanilla extract
½ cup sweetened shredded coconut
1 cup (4 oz.) chopped raw cashews, unsalted
1 cup (4 oz.) chopped dates
¼ cup (2 oz.) sweetened shredded coconut, reserved for topping

Yield: 2½ dozen

Sprinkle about a teaspoonful of coconut on top of each cookie before sliding the sheets into the oven. When the cookies have finished baking, the coconut will take on a golden, toasted color.

Lacy Oatmeal Cookies

1 cup quick oats
¼ cup all-purpose flour
½ tsp. salt
1½ tsp. baking powder
1 cup white sugar
½ cup salted butter, softened
1 large egg
1 tsp. pure vanilla extract

Yield: 8 dozen

Preheat oven to 325° F. Cover baking sheets with foil, then coat with a nonstick vegetable spray.

In a medium bowl combine oats, flour, salt and baking powder. Mix well with a wire whisk and set aside.

In a large bowl combine sugar and butter with an electric mixer at medium speed to form a grainy paste. Add egg and vanilla, and beat until smooth. Add flour mixture and blend just until combined.

Drop dough by teaspoonfuls onto baking sheets, 2½ inches apart. Bake for 10-12 minutes or until edges begin to turn golden brown. Let cool, then peel off cookies with fingers.

Be sure to respray baking sheets between batches.

Cocomia Cookies

Preheat oven to 300° F.

In a medium bowl combine flour, soda and salt. Mix well with a wire whisk and set aside.

In a large bowl blend sugars with an electric mixer at medium speed. Add butter and mix to form a grainy paste. Scrape down sides of bowl, then add eggs and vanilla. Beat at medium speed until light and fluffy.

Add the flour mixture, coconut and macadamia nuts, and blend at low speed just until combined. Do not overmix.

Drop by rounded tablespoons onto ungreased cookie sheets, 2 inches apart. Bake for 22-24 minutes. Immediately transfer cookies with a spatula to a cool, flat surface.

2 cups all-purpose flour
½ tsp. baking soda
¼ tsp. salt
¾ cup brown sugar, packed
½ cup white sugar
¾ cup salted butter, softened
2 large eggs
2 tsp. pure vanilla extract
1 cup (6 oz.) shredded,
unsweetened coconut
1½ cups (7 oz.) whole
macadamia nuts

Yield: 3 dozen

Applesauce Oaties

1¾ cups quick oats
1½ cup all-purpose flour
1 tsp. baking powder
½ tsp. baking soda
½ tsp. salt
1 tsp. ground cinnamon
½ tsp. ground nutmeg
1 cup light brown sugar, packed
½ cup white sugar
½ cup salted butter, softened
1 large egg
¾ cup applesauce
1 cup (6 oz.) semisweet
chocolate chips
1 cup (6 oz.) raisins
1 cup (4 oz.) chopped walnuts

Yield: 4 dozen

Preheat oven to 375° F.

In a medium bowl combine oats, flour, baking powder, soda, salt, cinnamon and nutmeg. Mix well with a wire whisk and set aside.

In a large bowl combine sugars with an electric mixer at medium speed. Add butter and beat to form a grainy paste. Add egg and applesauce, and blend until smooth.

Add the flour mixture, chocolate chips, raisins and walnuts. Blend at low speed just until combined. Do not overmix.

Drop dough by tablespoonfuls onto lightly greased baking sheets, 2 inches apart. Bake 12-14 minutes or until light brown. Immediately transfer cookies with a spatula to a cool, flat surface.

Fancy Cookies

Shortbread:
1½ cups salted butter, softened
1 cup confectioners' sugar
1 Tbsp. pure vanilla extract
3 cups all-purpose flour

Chocolate Glaze:
¼ cup heavy cream
1 cup (6 oz.) semisweet
chocolate chips
2 tsp. light corn syrup

Yield: 4 dozen

Preheat oven to 325° F.

Blend butter until smooth in a large bowl using an electric mixer set at medium speed. Slowly blend in the confectioners' sugar. Scrape down the sides of the bowl, then add vanilla extract and combine thoroughly. Add flour and mix at low speed until well blended.

Divide dough into two roughly equal pieces. Flatten each piece into a disk and wrap in plastic wrap. Refrigerate until firm, about 1½ hours.

On a floured board using a floured rolling pin, roll out disks to ⅛-inch thickness. Turn dough often to prevent sticking. Cut cookies with flour-dipped cookie cutters. Bake on ungreased cookie sheets for 16-18 minutes, being careful not to let the cookies brown. Transfer cookies immediately to a cool, flat surface with a spatula.

To prepare the chocolate glaze: Heat cream in a small saucepan until scalded; remove from heat. Stir in chocolate chips and corn syrup, cover, and let stand for 15 minutes. With small wire whisk or wooden spoon gently mix glaze until smooth, being careful not to create bubbles in the chocolate. Dip whole or half of each cookie into glaze and transfer to a tray or cool cookie sheet covered with waxed paper. Chill cookies in refrigerator for 10 minutes to set.

Bizcochitos

Preheat oven to 300° F.

Whisk together flour, baking soda, salt, and aniseed in a small bowl and set aside.

Blend sugars in a medium bowl using an electric mixer set at medium speed. Add butter, and mix until grainy, scraping down the sides of the bowl. Add eggs and brandy, and beat at medium speed until light and fluffy.

Add the flour mixture and mix at low speed until just combined. Do not overmix.

Roll rounded tablespoons of dough into 1-inch-diameter balls and then flatten each one slightly with the bottom of a glass or a spatula. Press tops into sugar-cinnamon mixture, then place them on ungreased cookie sheets, 1½ inches apart. Bake 22-24 minutes until cookies are slightly brown along edges.

Transfer cookies immediately to cool surface with a spatula.

Cookies:
2¾ cups all-purpose flour
½ tsp. baking soda
¼ tsp. salt
2½ tsp. aniseed
¾ cup light brown sugar, firmly packed
¾ cup white sugar
1 cup salted butter, softened
2 large eggs
2 tsp. brandy

Topping:
¼ cup white sugar
2 Tbsp. ground cinnamon

Yield: 3 dozen

Almond Crunch Cookies

½ cup salted butter, softened
¾ cup white sugar
1 large egg
½ tsp. pure almond extract
¼ cup (1 oz.) almonds, ground in blender or food processor
1 cup (4 oz.) sliced almonds
1 cup all-purpose flour
¼ cup heavy cream
1 cup (6 oz.) semisweet chocolate chips
2 tsp. light corn syrup

Yield: 1½ dozen

Preheat oven to 350° F.

In a medium bowl blend butter and sugar with an electric mixer until mixture forms a grainy paste. Scrape down sides of bowl, then add egg and almond extract. Beat at medium speed until light and fluffy.

Add the ground almonds and flour, and blend at low speed just until combined. Do not overmix. Form dough into 1½-inch balls and roll in sliced almonds, coating each ball thoroughly.

Place balls on ungreased cookie sheets, 2 inches apart. Bake for 15-18 minutes or until cookies are slightly brown along edges. Immediately transfer cookies to a cool surface covered with waxed paper.

To make the chocolate glaze: Scald cream in a small saucepan, then remove from heat. Stir in chocolate chips and corn syrup; cover and let stand for 15 minutes. With small wire whisk or wooden spoon, gently mix glaze until smooth, being careful not to create bubbles in the chocolate.

When cookies are completely cool, drizzle patterns on them with the warm chocolate glaze, or dip half of each cookie into the glaze. Refrigerate the cookies on the waxed paper until the glaze has set—about 10 minutes.

Roll dough lightly between your hands into 1½-inch balls (far left). The less you handle these cookies the lighter they will be. Then roll each ball in sliced almonds until fully coated (left).

48

Molasses Raisin Cookies

Preheat oven to 300° F.

In a medium bowl combine flour, soda, salt, cinnamon, ginger and allspice. Mix well with a wire whisk and set aside.

In a large bowl beat sugar and butter with an electric mixer at medium speed until mixture forms a grainy paste. Scrape sides of bowl, then add molasses and egg. Beat until light and fluffy.

Add the flour mixture and raisins, and blend at low speed just until combined. Do not overmix.

Divide dough in half and shape each half into a roll 1½ inches in diameter. Wrap rolls in waxed paper and refrigerate until firm, about 2 hours.

Slice cookies ½-inch thick and place on ungreased cookie sheets, 1½ inches apart. Bake for 25-27 minutes until cookies are set. Immediately transfer cookies with a spatula to a cool surface.

To prepare the icing: Blend sugar and milk in a small bowl until smooth. Using a small spoon or knife, drizzle cookies with icing.

Cookies:
3¼ cups all-purpose flour
1 tsp. baking soda
¼ tsp. salt
2 tsp. ground cinnamon
1 tsp. ground ginger
½ tsp. allspice
1 cup dark brown sugar, packed
1 cup salted butter, softened
¾ cup unsulfured molasses
1 large egg
1½ cups (6 oz.) raisins

Icing:
1 cup confectioners' sugar
2 Tbsp. milk

Yield: 4 dozen

Unwrap the chilled rolls of dough and slice with a sharp knife into ½-inch-thick cookies. Place on ungreased baking sheet.

Cinnamon Sugar Butter Cookies

Topping:
3 Tbsp. white sugar
1 Tbsp. ground cinnamon

Cookies:
2½ cups all-purpose flour
½ tsp. baking soda
¼ tsp. salt
1 cup dark brown sugar, packed
½ cup white sugar
1 cup salted butter, softened
2 large eggs
2 tsp. pure vanilla extract

Yield: 3 dozen

Preheat oven to 300° F.

In a small bowl combine sugar and cinnamon for topping. Set aside.

In a medium bowl combine flour, soda and salt. Mix well with a wire whisk and set aside.

In a large bowl blend sugars with an electric mixer set at medium speed. Add the butter, and mix to form a grainy paste. Scrape sides of bowl, then add the eggs and vanilla extract. Mix at medium speed until light and fluffy.

Add the flour mixture and blend at low speed just until combined. Do not overmix. Shape dough into 1-inch balls and roll each ball in cinnamon-sugar topping.

Place onto ungreased cookie sheets, 2 inches apart. Bake for 18-20 minutes. Immediately transfer cookies with a spatula to a cool, flat surface.

Gingersnaps

Preheat oven to 300° F.

In a medium bowl combine flour, soda, salt, ground ginger, crystallized ginger, allspice, and pepper. Mix well with a wire whisk. Set aside.

In a large bowl, mix sugar and butter with an electric mixer set at medium speed. Scrape down the sides of the bowl. Add egg and molasses, and beat at medium speed until light and fluffy.

Add the flour mixture and mix at low speed just until combined. Do not overmix. Chill the dough in the refrigerator for 1 hour—the dough will be less sticky and easier to handle.

Form dough into balls 1 inch in diameter. Place onto ungreased cookie sheets, 1½ inches apart. Bake 24-25 minutes. Use a spatula to immediately transfer cookies to a cool, flat surface.

2½ cups all-purpose flour
½ tsp. baking soda
¼ tsp. salt
2 tsp. ground ginger
1 tsp. diced crystallized ginger
½ tsp. allspice
½ tsp. ground black pepper
1¼ cups dark brown sugar, firmly packed
¾ cup salted butter, softened
1 large egg
¼ cup unsulfured molasses

Yield: 2½ dozen

Macadamia Nut Coconut Crisps

1 cup all-purpose flour
1 cup (4 oz.) raw macadamia nuts, coarsely chopped
½ cup shredded sweetened coconut
½ cup salted butter, softened
½ cup light corn syrup
½ cup dark brown sugar, firmly packed
2 tsp. pure vanilla extract
⅓ cup (2 oz.) miniature semisweet chocolate chips

Yield: 3 dozen

Preheat oven to 375° F.

Whisk together flour, nuts and coconut in a medium bowl. Set aside.

Heat butter, corn syrup and brown sugar in a 2-quart saucepan until boiling, stirring occasionally. Remove saucepan from heat and stir in vanilla. Add flour mixture and chocolate chips, and mix until all ingredients are equally distributed.

Drop by half teaspoonfuls onto well-greased cookie sheets, 2 inches apart. Bake 8-10 minutes or until mixture spreads and bubbles.

Cool cookies for 1 minute on pan, then immediately transfer to a cool, flat surface with a metal spatula. Cookies will remain soft until completely cooled.

Gently spoon the dry ingredients into the heated butter-and-sugar mixture (far left). Stir after every few spoonfuls until the dry ingredients are well incorporated (left).

Maple Pecan Butter Balls

Preheat oven to 300° F.

In a medium bowl combine flour, soda, cinnamon and finely ground pecans. (For extra flavor, saute pecans in 1 tablespoon butter until slightly browned.) Mix ingredients well with a wire whisk and set aside.

In a medium bowl cream butter and sugar with an electric mixer set at medium speed until mixture forms a grainy paste. Add syrup and egg and beat until slightly thickened.

Add the flour mixture and blend at low speed just until combined. Do not overmix. Place dough in plastic bag and refrigerate until firm, about 1 hour.

Remove dough from refrigerator and shape into 1-inch balls. Place cookies on ungreased cookie sheet, 1 inch apart. Bake 17-18 minutes, or until the cookie bottoms are golden brown. Immediately transfer cookies with a spatula to a cool, flat surface.

1¼ cups all-purpose flour
½ tsp. baking soda
1 tsp. ground cinnamon
¾ cup (3 oz.) pecans, finely ground in food processor or blender
½ cup salted butter, softened
⅔ cup white sugar
¼ cup pure maple syrup
1 large egg

Yield: 2 dozen

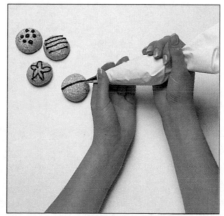

To make cookies more festive, sprinkle cookies with confectioners' sugar using a small mesh sieve (far left). Then, spoon chocolate icing into a pastry bag fitted with a small (#3) plain tip. Pipe decorative patterns onto cookies as shown (left).

Choconut Macaroons

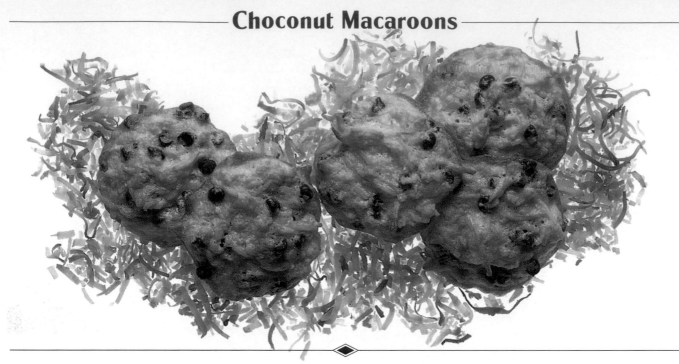

¼ *cup white sugar*
2 Tbsp. pure almond paste
(marzipan)
1 cup shredded sweetened coconut
⅓ *cup (2 oz.) miniature semisweet*
chocolate chips
3 large egg whites
½ *tsp. cream of tartar*

Yield: 1½ dozen

Preheat oven to 325° F.

Combine almond paste and sugar in a medium bowl. Using your fingers, work paste into sugar completely. Add coconut and chocolate chips and stir to combine.

In a clean medium-sized bowl beat egg whites until fluffy using absolutely clean beaters. Add cream of tartar and beat on high until stiff peaks form. Add half of beaten egg whites to coconut mixture and combine to lighten. Fold in remaining whites gently being careful not to deflate.

Drop by rounded teaspoons onto lightly greased cookie sheets. Bake 20 minutes until tops are lightly browned. Cool 1 minute on the cookie sheets before transferring cookies to a cool surface.

Spoon about half of the beaten egg whites into the cookie batter, and stir lightly but thoroughly until the egg whites are well combined (far left). Add the remaining egg whites and, using a spatula, bring the lightened batter up from the bottom of the bowl over the egg whites (left). Continue folding the egg whites into the batter just until they are incorporated. Be careful not to deflate the egg whites.

Cinnamon Maple Rings

Combine flour and sugar in a medium bowl using an electric mixer set on medium speed. Add butter and mix until the dough forms small, pea-sized pellets. Add chilled maple syrup and 2 tablespoons of water, and mix on low speed until dough can be formed into a ball. Do not overmix, or the pastry will be tough.

Separate dough into 2 balls and flatten into disks. Wrap dough tightly in plastic wrap or place in plastic bags. Refrigerate for 2 hours or until firm.

To prepare the filling: Combine sugar and cinnamon in small bowl.   Preheat oven to 325° F.

Using a floured rolling pin on a floured board, roll one piece of dough into a rough rectangle 10 inches wide, 15 inches long, and ⅛ inch thick. Sprinkle dough with half of the cinnamon-sugar filling. Starting with smaller side, roll dough up tightly into a cylinder. Dampen edge with water and seal. Repeat with remaining dough. Wrap each roll in plastic wrap and refrigerate for 1 hour.

Using a sharp thin knife, cut ¼-inch slices from each roll. Place slices on ungreased baking sheets, 1 inch apart. Brush tops lightly with ¼ cup maple syrup. Bake for 16-17 minutes or until light golden brown. Immediately transfer cookies to a cool, flat surface with spatula.

Pastry:
2 cups all-purpose flour
¼ cup white sugar
1 cup salted butter, chilled & sliced into 8 pieces
¼ cup pure maple syrup, chilled
2-4 Tbsp. ice water

Filling:
¼ cup white sugar
4 tsp. ground cinnamon

Topping:
¼ cup pure maple syrup

Yield: 4 dozen

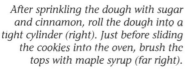

After sprinkling the dough with sugar and cinnamon, roll the dough into a tight cylinder (right). Just before sliding the cookies into the oven, brush the tops with maple syrup (far right).

Gingerbread Men

Cookies:
3¼ cups all-purpose flour
½ tsp. baking soda
¼ tsp. salt
1 tsp. ground cinnamon
2 tsp. ground ginger
¼ tsp. ground cloves
1 cup salted butter, softened
¾ cup dark brown sugar, firmly packed
1 large egg
½ cup unsulfured molasses
½ cup (3 oz.) raisins (optional)

Icing:
⅔ cup confectioners' sugar
1 to 2 tsp. milk

Yield: 2½ dozen 6-inch cookies
3½ dozen 4-inch cookies

Preheat oven to 325° F.

Whisk together flour, soda, salt, cinnamon, ginger, and cloves in a medium bowl.

In large bowl with an electric mixer cream butter and sugar. Scrape down the sides of the bowl. Add egg and molasses, and beat on medium speed until smooth. Scrape bowl and add the flour mixture. Blend on low speed just until combined; do not overmix.

Separate dough into 2 balls and flatten into disks. Wrap each disk tightly in plastic wrap or a plastic bag, and refrigerate 1 hour or until firm.

On floured surface with floured rolling pin, roll dough out to ¼ inch thickness. With floured cookie cutters cut into gingerbread men. Gather scraps and reroll dough until all dough is used. Place on ungreased baking sheets ½ inch apart.

If you want to use raisins to decorate the cookies, plump raisins first by soaking them in warm water for 5 minutes. Discard water. Use raisins as eyes, mouths and buttons.

Bake 9-11 minutes being careful not to brown. Transfer to cool flat surface with spatula.

To prepare the icing: Whisk sugar and milk together in a small bowl until mixture is smooth but liquid. If it seems dry, add ¼ teaspoon more milk. Spoon icing into a pastry bag fitted with a small piping tip. Decorate gingerbread men as desired.

Christmas Sugar Cookies

Preheat oven to 325° F.

In a medium bowl combine the flour and salt with a wire whisk.

In a large mixing bowl cream the butter and sugar with an electric mixer on medium speed. Add the egg and vanilla, and beat until well mixed. Scrape down sides of bowl, then add the flour mixture. Blend on low speed just until combined. Do not overmix.

Gather dough into a ball. Flatten the ball into a disk and wrap tightly in plastic wrap or a plastic bag. Refrigerate 1 hour until firm.

On a floured surface, roll out dough to a ¼-inch thickness. With cookie cutters, cut dough into desired shapes and place on ungreased cookie sheets. Decorate with colored sugars or sprinkles.

Bake for 13-15 minutes, being careful not to brown. Immediately transfer cookies with a spatula to a cool, flat surface.

2 cups all-purpose flour
¼ tsp. salt
¾ cup salted butter, softened
¾ cup white sugar
1 large egg
1 tsp. pure vanilla extract
Colored sugars or other decorations

Yield: 3 dozen cookies

Brown Buttercrunch Cookies

Really Good!

Cookies:
½ cup salted butter, softened
½ cup corn syrup
⅔ cup dark brown sugar, packed
1 cup old-fashioned oats
(not quick or instant)
¾ cup all-purpose flour
1 tsp. pure vanilla

Chocolate Glaze:
¼ cup heavy cream
1 cup (6 oz.) semisweet
chocolate chips
2 tsp. light corn syrup

Yield: 2½ dozen

Preheat oven to 375° F. Line cookie sheets with parchment paper.

In a medium saucepan, melt butter, corn syrup and brown sugar over moderate heat, stirring constantly until sugar dissolves. Increase heat to high. When mixture boils remove from heat and stir in oats, flour and vanilla.

Bake cookies one pan at a time and be ready to work fast. Drop by half teaspoonfuls 3 inches apart onto paper-lined cookie sheets. Bake for 8 minutes or until mixture spreads, bubbles and begins to brown. Let cookies cool for 1-2 minutes before rolling.

Roll widest edge of cookie around a pencil or wooden spoon handle, creating a tube. Repeat with remaining cookies. If cookies become too brittle to roll, return to oven for about 30 seconds to soften. Cool rolled cookies completely.

To make the chocolate glaze: Heat cream in a small saucepan until scalded. Remove from heat and stir in chocolate chips and corn syrup. Cover and let stand about 15 minutes until chocolate has melted. Using a wire whisk or wooden spoon, gently mix glaze until smooth, being careful not to create bubbles.

When cookies are cool, dip all or half of each cookie into the glaze and transfer back to parchment paper. Refrigerate for 10-15 minutes to set.

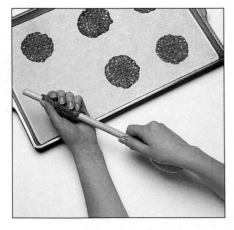

Wrap the warm cookie around a wooden spoon handle (far left). If cookie cools too much, it may crack when rolled. Dip half of each rolled cookie in melted chocolate and return to cookie sheet (left).

Preheat oven to 375° F. Line cookie sheets with waxed paper.

In a double boiler melt the unsweetened chocolate and the first batch of chocolate chips. Stir frequently with wooden spoon or wire whisk until creamy and smooth.

Pour melted chocolate into a large bowl. Add butter and beat with electric mixer at medium speed until thoroughly combined.

Add the sugar, eggs and vanilla. Beat on medium speed until well blended. Scrape down sides of bowl.

Add the flour and the three types of chocolate chips. Mix at low speed just until combined. Chips should be distributed equally throughout the dough.

Roll a heaping tablespoon of dough into a ball, about 1½ inches in diameter. Place dough balls onto paper-lined pans, 2 inches apart. With the palm of your hand, flatten each ball to ½-inch thickness.

Bake for 10-12 minutes. Transfer cookies with a spatula to a cool, flat surface.

2 oz. unsweetened chocolate
¾ cup (4 oz.) semisweet chocolate chips
½ cup salted butter, softened
1 cup white sugar
2 large eggs
2 tsp. pure vanilla extract
1½ cups all-purpose flour
1 cup (6 oz.) semisweet chocolate chips
½ cup (3 oz.) white chocolate chips
¼ cup (1.5 oz.) milk chocolate chips

Yield: 2½ dozen

¾ cup salted butter, softened
⅓ cup white sugar
1 tsp. pure vanilla extract
¼ tsp. pure almond extract
1 cup all-purpose flour
1 cup (6 oz.) semisweet
  chocolate chips
1 cup (4 oz.) slivered almonds

Yield: 2 dozen

Preheat oven to 350° F.

Cream butter and sugar together in a medium bowl using an electric mixer set at medium speed. Add extracts and beat well. Scrape bowl. Add flour, chocolate chips and almonds, and blend on low speed until just combined. Do not overmix.

Shape rounded tablespoonfuls into 1½-inch balls and place on ungreased baking sheets, 2 inches apart. Press balls with palm of hand or bottom of drinking glass into ½-inch-thick rounds.

Bake 15-17 minutes or until cookies just begin to brown. Transfer cookies to a cool, flat surface.

Snowy White Chocolate Crescents

Preheat oven to 325° F.

In a small bowl combine flour and cocoa. Mix well with a wire whisk and set aside.

In a medium bowl cream butter and sugar with an electric mixer on medium speed. Add vanilla and egg, and beat until light and smooth. Scrape down sides of bowl, then add flour and cocoa mixture. Blend on low speed until fully incorporated. The dough will be dry and crumbly.

Shape a level tablespoonful of dough into a 3½-inch log. Slightly bend the log to form a crescent shape. Form remaining dough into crescents, and place on ungreased baking sheets, 1 inch apart. Bake 15-17 minutes or until the outside of cookie is hard but the center remains soft.

Cool on pan for 2-3 minutes, then transfer to a flat surface to cool a few minutes more. While still warm, roll the cookies in confectioners' sugar until coated.

1½ cups all-purpose flour
⅓ cup cocoa powder, unsweetened
½ cup salted butter, softened
1 cup white sugar
1 tsp. pure vanilla extract
1 large egg
½ cup confectioners' sugar

Yield: 2½ dozen

To form the chocolate cookies, roll dough briskly between your hands into 3½-inch logs (far left). Then bend each log slightly to form a crescent shape (left) and bake.

Apple Cobbler Cookies

Cookies:
3 cups all-purpose flour
1 tsp. baking powder
1 tsp. ground cinnamon
½ cup white sugar
½ cup light brown sugar, firmly packed
1 cup salted butter, softened
2 large eggs
2 tsp. pure vanilla extract
¼ cup apple juice
½ cup apple butter
1 cup tart apples, peeled and chopped
1 cup (6 oz.) raisins
1 cup (4 oz.) pecans, finely chopped

Crumb Coating:
1¼ cups light brown sugar, firmly packed
1½ cups quick oats (not instant)
1¼ tsp. ground cinnamon
9 Tbsp. salted butter, melted

Yield: 4 dozen

Preheat oven to 300° F.

In medium bowl combine flour, baking powder and cinnamon. Mix well with wire whisk. Set aside.

Combine sugars in a large bowl. Add butter and mix using an electric mixer set at medium speed, scraping down the sides of the bowl. Add eggs and vanilla, and blend until smooth. Thoroughly incorporate the apple juice and apple butter. Add the flour mixture, chopped apples, raisins and pecans, and blend at low speed until just combined. Do not overmix.

To prepare the crumb coating: Combine sugar, oats and cinnamon in medium bowl. Mix well with a wire whisk. Add melted butter and mix until dry ingredients are well moistened. Set aside.

Roll dough into 1-inch-diameter balls. Roll each ball in crumb mixture until well coated. Place cookies on ungreased cookie sheets, 2 inches apart. Bake 24-26 minutes, or until cookie is firm to the touch and crumb mixture begins to brown. Transfer to a cool, flat surface with spatula.

Roll each ball of dough in the crumb coating until it is completely covered. It may be necessary to press the mixture into the dough to make sure it sticks. Place the coated balls on ungreased cookie sheets and bake as directed.

Russian Tea Cakes

Preheat oven to 325° F.

In a large bowl cream butter and sugar using an electric mixer. Add vanilla, scraping down bowl as needed. Blend in flour and salt, mixing until thoroughly combined.

Roll tablespoonfuls of dough into small balls about 1 inch in diameter. Place dough balls on lightly greased cookie sheets about 1 inch apart. Press down the center of each ball with a spoon, forming a depression. Fill each with a teaspoonful of preserves or nuts.

Bake 15-20 minutes or until golden brown. Transfer cookies immediately to a cool, flat surface. When cookies are completely cool, dust them lightly with confectioners' sugar.

Cookies:
1 cup salted butter
½ cup confectioners' sugar
2 tsp. pure vanilla extract
2 cups all-purpose flour
¼ tsp. salt

Topping:
½ cup fruit preserves or
½ cup (2 oz.) chopped walnuts
¼ cup confectioners' sugar

Yield: 2 dozen

Shortbread:
1 cup salted butter, softened
¾ cup light brown sugar, packed
2 tsp. pure vanilla extract
2 cups all-purpose flour

Topping:
1 tbsp. salted butter
1 cup (6 oz.) semisweet
chocolate chips
1 cup (4 oz.) pecans, finely chopped

Yield: 2½ dozen

Preheat oven to 325° F.

In a large bowl cream butter and sugar with an electric mixer at medium speed. Scrape down sides of bowl. Then add vanilla and flour, and blend thoroughly on low speed.

Shape level tablespoonfuls of dough into 1-inch balls, then form into logs 2 inches long and 1 inch wide. Place on ungreased baking sheets, 2 inches apart.

Bake for 17-19 minutes or until cookies spread and turn a light golden brown. Transfer to a cool, flat surface.

To make topping: Melt butter and chocolate chips in a double boiler over hot (not boiling) water or in a microwave oven on high power. Stir chocolate every 30 seconds until melted.

Dip top of each cooled shortbread cookie into melted chocolate, then into chopped pecans. Place cookies on waxed paper and refrigerate to set.

Keeping bowls of topping close to the cookie sheet, dip the top of each cooled shortbread cookie into the melted chocolate (far left) and then into the chopped pecans (left). Place on cookie sheet lined with waxed paper and chill.

Filled Cookies

Chocolate Cream-Filled Hearts

Cookies:
1½ cups salted butter, softened
1½ cups confectioners' sugar
4 tsp. pure vanilla extract
3 cups all-purpose flour

Chocolate Cream Filling:
½ cup heavy cream
1 cup (6 oz.) semisweet chocolate chips

Topping:
¼ cup confectioners' sugar

Yield: 2½ dozen cookies

Cream butter in a medium bowl with electric mixer set at medium speed. Add 1½ cups confectioners' sugar and beat until smooth. Add vanilla and mix until creamy. Scrape bowl. Add flour and mix at low speed until thoroughly mixed.

Gather dough into 2 balls and flatten to disks. Wrap dough tightly in plastic wrap or place in an airtight plastic bag. Refrigerate for 1 hour or until firm.

Preheat oven to 325° F.

Using a floured rolling pin, roll dough on floured board to ¼-inch thickness. Cut out 2-inch hearts with cookie cutters. Continue using dough scraps, rerolling and recutting until all dough is used. Be careful not to overwork the dough.

Place cookies on ungreased cookie sheet, ½ inch apart. Bake 16-18 minutes or until firm. Transfer to cool, flat surface with spatula.

To prepare the chocolate cream filling: Scald the cream in a small saucepan and remove from heat. Stir in the chocolate chips and cover for 15 minutes. Stir chocolate cream until smooth, then transfer to a small bowl. Set filling aside and let it cool to room temperature.

Spread 1 teaspoonful of chocolate filling on the bottom side of half of the cookies. Top with bottom side of another cookie, forming a sandwich. Repeat with remaining cookies and cream.

If you wish, sift confectioners' sugar over the finished cookies.

Spread the chocolate filling on the bottom side of one cookie heart. Top with another heart, bottom side also touching the chocolate.

Chocolate Sandwich Cookies

Really Good!!

In a medium bowl cream butter with an electric mixer at medium speed. Add sugar and beat until smooth. Add vanilla and beat at medium speed until light and fluffy. In another bowl, combine the cocoa, cornstarch and flour, and mix well with a wire whisk. Add the cocoa mixture to the wet ingredients and mix at low speed until thoroughly combined.

Gather dough into a ball and flatten into a disk. Wrap dough tightly in plastic wrap or place in an airtight plastic bag. Refrigerate for 1½ hours or until firm.

Preheat oven to 325° F.

Using a floured rolling pin, roll dough on floured board to ¼-inch thickness. Cut shapes with cookie cutters and place on ungreased cookie sheets, 1 inch apart. Continue using dough scraps, rerolling and cutting until all dough is used. Be careful not to overwork the dough. Bake 16-18 minutes or until firm. Transfer cookies to a cool, flat surface with spatula.

To prepare the cream filling: Cream butter in a small bowl with an electric mixer set at medium speed. Add sugar, vanilla and cream, and beat until smooth.

Spread 1½ teaspoons of cream filling on the bottom sides of half of the cookies. Top with the remaining cookies.

Cookies:
¾ cup salted butter, softened
¾ cup confectioners' sugar
2 tsp. pure vanilla extract
¼ cup unsweetened cocoa powder
2 Tbsp. cornstarch
1 cup all-purpose flour

Cream Filling:
½ cup salted butter, softened
1 cup confectioners' sugar
2 tsp. pure vanilla extract
1 Tbsp. heavy cream

Yield: 1½ dozen

¾ cup salted butter, softened
½ cup confectioner's sugar
2 large egg yolks
1 tsp. pure vanilla
1½ cups all-purpose flour
1 cup any fresh fruit jam

Yield: 2 dozen

Preheat oven to 325° F.

In a medium bowl cream butter with an electric mixer set at medium speed. Add sugar and beat until smooth. Add egg yolks and vanilla, and beat at medium speed until light and fluffy. Add the flour and blend at low speed until thoroughly combined.

Gather dough into a ball and flatten to a disk. Wrap dough tightly in plastic wrap or place in plastic bag. Refrigerate for 1 hour.

Using a floured rolling pin, roll dough on floured board to ¼-inch thickness. Cut circles with a 2-inch-diameter cookie cutter or drinking glass, and place on ungreased cookie sheets, 1 inch apart. Continue using dough scraps, rerolling and cutting until all dough is used.

Drop ½ teaspoon of fruit jam in center of each cookie, then top with another cookie. Using the tines of a fork, seal edges of cookies as shown.

Bake for 15-17 minutes or until edges begin to brown.

Chocolate Dreams

In a medium bowl cream butter using an electric mixer set at medium speed. Add confectioners' and brown sugars and beat until smooth. Add yolks and vanilla, and mix at medium speed until light and fluffy. Scrape bowl. Add the flour and blend at low speed until thoroughly combined.

Gather dough into a ball and flatten to a disk. Wrap dough tightly in plastic wrap or place in plastic bag. Refrigerate for one hour.

To prepare the filling: Scald the cream in a small saucepan over medium heat. Add the chocolate chips and stir until melted. Remove from the heat.

Preheat oven to 325° F.

Using a floured rolling pin, roll dough on floured board to ¼-inch thickness. Cut circles with a 2-inch-diameter cookie cutter and place on ungreased cookie sheets, 1 inch apart. Continue using dough scraps, rerolling and cutting until all dough is used. Drop 1 teaspoon of chocolate filling in center of each circle and top with another circle. Completely seal the edges using the tines of a fork. Bake 15-16 minutes, or until cookies are golden brown. Transfer cookies to a cool, flat surface with a metal spatula. Sprinkle with white sugar, if desired.

Cookies:
¾ cup salted butter, softened
½ cup confectioners' sugar
¼ cup light brown sugar, firmly packed
2 large egg yolks
1 tsp. pure vanilla extract
1½ cups all-purpose flour

Chocolate Filling:
½ cup heavy cream
1 cup (6 oz.) semisweet chocolate chips

Topping:
2 Tbsp. white sugar

Yield: 2½ dozen

Spoon a heaping teaspoonful of chocolate filling into the center of each circle (far left). Cover each with another circle of dough and completely seal the edges with a fork (left).

Custard:
1 cup sweetened condensed milk
one ½-inch piece vanilla bean split
lengthwise or 1 tsp. pure vanilla
extract
2 large egg yolks, room temperature

Cookies:
½ cup salted butter, softened
½ cup white sugar
1 large egg
2 Tbsp. heavy cream
1½ cups all-purpose flour

Topping:
1 tsp. ground cinnamon or
1 tsp. confectioners' sugar or
1 tsp. cocoa powder

Yield: 1½ dozen

In a medium saucepan over medium heat, heat condensed milk with vanilla bean or vanilla extract until small bubbles form on surface.

Whisk egg yolks in a medium bowl. Stirring constantly, slowly add ½ cup of the hot milk to the egg yolks. Add the tempered egg yolks to the milk mixture in the saucepan. Stirring constantly with a metal spoon or whisk, cook for 5 minutes or until custard heavily coats the back of a spoon. Be careful not to let the custard boil.

Strain custard through a sieve. Refrigerate until thoroughly chilled.

Preheat oven to 325° F.

To prepare the cookies: Mix butter and sugar in medium bowl with electric mixer at medium speed. Add egg and cream and mix until thoroughly blended. Scrape sides of bowl. Add the flour and blend on low speed just until combined. Do not overmix.

Shape dough into 1-inch balls and place on ungreased cookie sheets 1 inch apart. With your thumb or the back of a small spoon, form a small depression in center of each ball.

Bake 15-17 minutes or until bottoms begin to brown. Transfer cookies to cool, flat surface. When cookies cool to room temperature, spoon or pipe in 1½ teaspoons of chilled thickened custard. Sprinkle with ground cinnamon, confectioners' sugar or cocoa, if desired.

Temper the beaten egg yolks by adding about ½ cup of the hot milk into the yolks, briskly whisking as you pour. This will warm the eggs enough so that when you add them to the hot milk, they will not become scrambled eggs.

Linzer Cookies

Preheat oven to 300° F.

In medium bowl combine flour, almonds, baking powder, salt and cinnamon with wire whisk.

In large bowl with an electric mixer cream butter and sugar. Add egg yolks, the vanilla and almond extracts, and beat at medium speed until light and fluffy. Add the flour mixture and blend at low speed until just combined. Do not overmix.

Roll dough into 1½-inch balls. Place 2 inches apart on ungreased baking sheet. With index finger press an indentation in center of each ball to hold the filling.

Bake 22-24 minutes or until just golden brown on bottom. Transfer cookies to a cool, flat surface with spatula.

In a small bowl combine jam and grated lemon peel. Place ½ teaspoon of filling mixture in center of cooled cookie. If you wish to add an extra decorative touch, sift confectioners' sugar over cookies and place sliced almonds in the jam filling.

Cookies:
1½ cups all-purpose flour
½ cup ground almonds
½ tsp. baking powder
¼ tsp. salt
½ tsp. ground cinnamon
¾ cup salted butter, softened
¾ cup white sugar
2 egg yolks
1 tsp. pure vanilla extract
1 tsp. pure almond extract

Filling:
½ cup raspberry jam
1 tsp. grated lemon peel
(half of medium lemon)

Topping:
¼ cup confectioners' sugar
½ cup (2 oz.) sliced almonds

Yield: 2 dozen

Once the cookies are cool, lightly dust them with confectioners' sugar (far left). Next, spoon the raspberry jam into the depression in each cookie. To finish off, arrange sliced almonds on top of the jam (left).

Pineapple Pocket Pies

Cookies:
1 cup all-purpose flour
½ cup whole wheat flour
½ tsp. baking soda
¼ cup salted butter, softened
¼ cup light brown sugar,
firmly packed
¼ cup honey
1 large egg
1 tsp. pure vanilla extract

Filling:
½ cup dried apricots
½ cup fresh or canned unsweetened
pineapple, in chunks
¼ cup dark brown sugar, firmly
packed
1½ cups water

Yield: 32 pockets

In medium bowl combine flours and soda. Mix well with a wire whisk. Set aside.

In large bowl with an electric mixer combine butter and sugar at medium speed. Add honey, egg and vanilla and beat at medium speed until smooth. Scrape down the sides of the bowl, then add the flour mixture. Blend at low speed until just combined; do not overmix.

Gather dough into a ball. Divide in half and roll into two 6-inch cylinders. Wrap each cylinder tightly in plastic wrap or in a plastic bag. Refrigerate 1 hour.

To prepare the filling: Combine all the filling ingredients in medium saucepan over medium-low heat and stir until sugar dissolves. Turn heat up to medium and simmer—stirring occasionally—until mixture thickens and most of the liquid evaporates. Remove from heat and allow mixture to cool to room temperature. Purée filling in food processor or blender.

Preheat oven to 325° F. Using your hands, roll each cylinder out to about 12 inches in length. Then place one cylinder on a floured board and using a floured rolling pin, roll into a rectangle roughly 5 inches wide, 18 inches long, and ⅛ inch thick.

Spread half of the filling mixture down the center of the dough in a ribbon about 2 inches wide. With metal spatula loosen the dough, and fold each side lengthwise over the filling, one side overlapping the other by ½ inch.

Cut strip in half widthwise to make handling easier. Use spatula to transfer each 9-inch strip onto an ungreased baking sheet, turning the strips over so that the seams are on the bottom. Repeat procedure with remaining dough and filling.

Bake 20-22 minutes or until dough begins to turn a light gold. Do not brown. Cool strips on sheet for 1 minute, then transfer to cool surface. When strips reach room temperature, cut each one into 8 pieces with a thin, sharp knife.

Refrigerator Thumbprint Fudgy Cookies

In a 2-quart saucepan combine butter, cream and sugar. Warm over medium heat until sugar dissolves. Remove from heat, add vanilla and chocolate chips, one cup at a time, stirrring until chocolate melts. To complete the dough, fold in the oats and stir until all ingredients are thoroughly combined.

Shape dough into 1-inch balls and place on a cookie sheet lined with waxed paper. Using the bottom of a glass, flatten cookies to 2 inches in diameter. Make a depression in center of each cookie with your thumb. Chill cookies in refrigerator 30 minutes or until set. Spoon one-half teaspoon of preserves into center of each cookie. Dust with confectioners' sugar.

¼ cup salted butter, softened
½ cup heavy cream
1 cup white sugar
1 tsp. pure vanilla extract
2 cups (12 oz.) semisweet chocolate chips
2½ cups quick oatmeal (not instant)
1 cup raspberry preserves
¼ cup confectioners' sugar

Yield: 2½ dozen

Spoon the chocolate chips into the liquid ingredients one cup at a time (far left). Stir after each addition to ensure that the chips have melted. After all the chocolate has been incorporated, add the oats and stir until completely moistened (left).

Apple Cream Pennies

Cookies:
2½ cups all-purpose flour
½ tsp. baking soda
¼ tsp. salt
1 cup dark brown sugar, firmly packed
½ cup white sugar
1 cup salted butter, softened
2 large eggs
2 tsp. pure vanilla extract

Filling:
8 oz. cream cheese, softened
¼ cup white sugar
¼ cup apple butter

Yield: 6 dozen

Preheat oven to 300° F.

In a medium bowl combine flour, soda and salt. Mix well with a wire whisk. Set aside.

Blend sugars in a large bowl using an electric mixer set at medium speed. Add butter and mix to form a grainy paste, scraping down the sides of the bowl. Add eggs and vanilla, and beat at medium speed until light and fluffy.

Add the flour mixture and blend at low speed until just combined. Do not overmix.

Shape dough into marble-sized balls. Place balls on ungreased baking sheets, 1 inch apart. Bake 10-11 minutes. Do not brown. Transfer cookies to a cool flat surface with a spatula.

To prepare the filling: Blend cream cheese and sugar in medium bowl with an electric mixer on medium until fluffy. Add apple butter and beat until smooth and thoroughly combined.

With a small knife spread 1 teaspoonful of apple cream on the bottom half of each cooled cookie. Top with another cookie to create a sandwich. Repeat with remaining cookies and filling.

Jessica's Marshmallow Clouds

Preheat oven to 400° F. Until you are ready to assemble the cookies just prior to baking, keep the marshmallows in the freezer—otherwise they will thaw too rapidly.

In medium bowl combine flour, cocoa and baking soda. Set aside.

Combine sugars in a large bowl. Using an electric mixer, blend in butter, scraping down the sides of the bowl. Add eggs and vanilla, and beat at medium speed until light and fluffy.

Add the flour mixture and chocolate chips, and blend at low speed until combined. Batter will be very stiff.

Gather 4-5 frozen marshmallows in the palm of your hand and cover them with a heaping tablespoonful of dough. Wrap the dough around the marshmallows, completely encasing them and forming a 2-inch-diameter dough ball.

Place balls on ungreased baking sheets, 2 inches apart. Bake 8-10 minutes. Cool on pan 2 minutes, then transfer to a cool, flat surface.

3 cups all-purpose flour
⅔ cup unsweetened cocoa powder
½ tsp. baking soda
1 cup white sugar
1 cup light brown sugar, firmly packed
1 cup salted butter, softened
2 large eggs
2 tsp. pure vanilla extract
2 cups (12 oz.) miniature semisweet chocolate chips
8 oz. miniature marshmallows, frozen

Yield: 3½ dozen

Take 4-5 frozen miniature marshmallows into the palm of your hand (far left). Spoon a heaping tablespoon of dough over the marshmallows and wrap them inside (left). Form a 2-inch ball, then place on an ungreased cookie sheet.

Surprise-Filled Cookies

2½ cups all-purpose flour
½ tsp. baking powder
1 cup salted butter, softened
1 cup white sugar
1 large egg
2 tsp. pure vanilla extract
1 cup fruit jam

Yield: 4 dozen

Preheat oven to 300° F.

In medium bowl combine flour and baking powder. Mix well with a wire whisk. Set aside.

In medium bowl with an electric mixer cream butter and sugar. Add egg and vanilla and beat on medium until smooth. Add the flour mixture and blend at low speed until thoroughly combined. Dough will be firm.

Scoop tablespoonfuls of dough, roll into 1-inch-diameter balls and place on ungreased baking sheets, 1 inch apart. With the small end of a melon baller, scoop out the center of the dough balls. Do not scoop all the way through the cookie. Place ½ teaspoon of jam in the center of each dough ball. Place scooped-out dough back into mixing bowl to use to form more cookies.

Bake 22-24 minutes or until light golden brown. Transfer to a cool, flat surface.

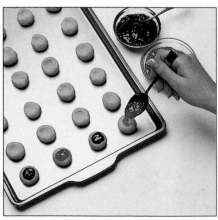

Use the smaller scoop of a melon baller to remove a small amount of dough from each ball (far left). Spoon your favorite jams into the depression (left), then bake as directed.

Peanut Butter Cream-Filled Cookies

Preheat oven to 325° F.

In medium bowl combine flour, soda, cinnamon and oats. Mix well with a wire whisk. Set aside.

Cream sugar and butter in a large bowl using an electric mixer set at medium speed. Add egg and vanilla, and beat at medium speed until light and creamy. Add the flour-oat mixture, and blend at low speed until just combined. Do not overmix.

Separate dough into two balls, flatten them into disks, and wrap each tightly in plastic wrap or a plastic bag. Chill 1 hour.

On floured board using a floured rolling pin, roll out one disk to ¼ inch thickness. Cut cookies with a 2-inch round fluted cookie cutter dipped in flour. Repeat procedure with the second disk, reworking scraps until all the dough is used. Bake cookies on ungreased baking sheets ½ inch apart for 13-15 minutes or until bottoms turn light brown. Transfer immediately to a cool, flat surface with a spatula.

When cookies are cool, spread 1 tablespoon of peanut butter filling on the bottom side of a cookie. Top with another cookie—bottom side toward the filling—to make a sandwich. Repeat with the remaining cookies and filling.

Cookies:
1½ cups all-purpose flour
½ tsp. baking soda
½ tsp. ground cinnamon
1 cup quick oats (not instant)
1 cup light brown sugar,
firmly packed
½ cup salted butter, softened
1 large egg
1 tsp. pure vanilla extract

Filling:
¾ cup smooth peanut butter
¼ cup salted butter, softened
2 Tbsp. half-and-half
1 tsp. pure vanilla extract
1½ cups confectioners' sugar

Yield: 3½ dozen

Use a cookie cutter dipped in flour to cut the cookies from the dough. This cookie cutter has a fluted edge—it makes a particularly attractive cookie.

Lemon Cream-Filled Cookies

Cookies:
¾ cup salted butter, softened
½ cup confectioners' sugar
2 tsp. pure lemon extract
1½ cups all-purpose flour
¼ cup cornstarch

Filling:
¼ cup salted butter, softened
1 cup confectioners' sugar
1 Tbsp. heavy cream
Juice of 1 freshly squeezed lemon
(about 2 Tbsp.)
Grated zest of 1 lemon (2-3 tsp.)

To make the cookie dough: In a medium bowl cream butter with an electric mixer set at medium speed. Add sugar, and beat until smooth, scraping down sides of bowl as needed.

Add lemon extract, and beat until light and fluffy. Then add flour and cornstarch; blend at low speed until thoroughly combined.

Gather dough into 2 balls of equal size and flatten into disks. Wrap the disks tightly in plastic wrap or a plastic bag. Refrigerate for 1 hour.

To make the filling: In a small bowl beat butter with mixer until fluffy. Gradually add sugar while continuing to beat. Add cream, lemon juice and lemon zest. Mix until thoroughly blended and set aside. To harden filling quickly, refrigerate for 15-20 minutes.

At this point, preheat the oven to 325° F.

Using a floured rolling pin, roll the chilled cookie dough on a floured board to ¼-inch thickness. Cut circles with a 2-inch-diameter cookie cutter or drinking glass. Place circles of dough on ungreased cookie sheets, ½-inch apart. Continue rolling out and cutting dough scraps until all dough is used.

Bake for 15-17 minutes, or until edges begin to brown. Immediately transfer cookies with a spatula to a cool, flat surface.

When cookies are completely cool, spread a cookie with 1 teaspoon of the lemon cream. Place another cookie on top of the filling to make a sandwich. Complete entire batch.

Bar Cookies

Blue-Ribbon Chocolate Chip Cookies:
2½ cups all-purpose flour
½ tsp. baking soda
¼ tsp. salt
1 cup dark brown sugar, packed
½ cup white sugar
1 cup salted butter, softened
2 large eggs
2 tsp. pure vanilla extract
2 cups (12 oz.) semisweet
chocolate chips
1 cup sweetened, shredded coconut

Double-Rich Chocolate Cookies:
1¼ cups all-purpose flour
¼ tsp. baking soda
⅛ tsp. salt
¼ cup unsweetened cocoa powder
½ cup dark brown sugar, packed
¼ cup + 2 Tbsp. white sugar
½ cup salted butter, softened
1 large egg
1 large egg yolk
1 tsp. pure vanilla extract
1 cup (6 oz.) semisweet chocolate
chips

Yield: 24 bars

After pressing the Chocolate Chip dough into the pan, sprinkle evenly with coconut. Then dollop the Double-Rich chocolate dough on top to resemble bull's eyes when cut.

Preheat oven to 300° F and grease a 9-by-13-inch glass baking dish.

First, make the Blue-Ribbon Cookies: In a medium bowl combine flour, soda, and salt. Mix well with a wire whisk.

In a large bowl blend sugars and butter with an electric mixer. Scrape sides of bowl, then add eggs and vanilla extract. Beat at medium speed until light and fluffy. Add flour mixture and chocolate chips, and mix just until combined. Press dough evenly into prepared pan and sprinkle with coconut. Set aside.

Next, make the Double-Rich Cookies: In a medium bowl combine flour, soda, salt and cocoa powder with a wire whisk.

In a large bowl blend sugars and butter with mixer at medium speed. Scrape bowl, then add eggs and vanilla, and beat until well combined. Add the flour mixture and chocolate chips, and blend on low. Do not overmix.

Drop the Double-Rich dough by rounded teaspoonfuls onto the Blue-Ribbon dough. Evenly space the darker dough on top of the lighter dough to resemble bull's eyes. Bake 50-60 minutes, until a toothpick inserted in center comes out clean. Cool and cut.

Creamy Layered Pudding Bar

Preheat oven to 325° F. Grease an 8-by-8-inch square baking pan.

In a medium bowl cream the butter and sugar at medium speed, scraping down the sides of the bowl. Add single egg yolk and vanilla and beat at medium speed until light and fluffy. Add the flour and the salt, and blend at low speed until just combined.

Turn dough out into prepared pan, and place in refrigerator for 15 minutes. When dough is chilled, lightly flour your hands and press the dough to ¼-inch thickness on bottom and sides of pan. Dough should extend 1 inch up sides of pan. Return pan to refrigerator while you prepare the filling.

To prepare the filling: Combine sugar and cornstarch in a small bowl. Mix well with a wire whisk. Set aside.

In a medium bowl with an electric mixer set on medium-high speed, beat the 5 egg yolks 5 minutes or until they are light and fluffy. Add cornstarch-sugar mixture and mix on medium until combined. Add the vanilla, whipping cream, chocolate chips and pecans and blend at low speed—scraping bowl as needed—until thoroughly combined. Pour filling into pastry-lined pan.

Bake 55-60 minutes or until filling is set and golden brown. Chill 4 hours or overnight. Cut into 16 bars and serve.

Crust:
½ cup salted butter, softened
¼ cup white sugar
1 large egg yolk
1 tsp. pure vanilla extract
1 cup cake flour
⅛ tsp. salt

Filling:
½ cup white sugar
1 Tbsp. cornstarch
5 large egg yolks
1 tsp. pure vanilla extract
1 cup whipping cream
1 cup (6 oz.) miniature semisweet chocolate chips
1 cup (4 oz.) pecans, chopped

Yield: 16 squares

Press the chilled dough firmly into the bottom of a greased 8-by-8-inch pan. The dough should extend up the sides of the pan by about an inch. Lightly flour your hands before you begin to prevent the dough from sticking to them.

Filling:
1½ cups (8 oz.) chopped dates
½ cup shredded sweetened coconut
¾ cup half-and-half or light cream
1 tsp. pure vanilla extract

Granola Base:
2 cups quick oats (not instant)
¾ cup all-purpose flour
1 cup dark brown sugar,
firmly packed
½ tsp. baking soda
½ tsp. ground cinnamon
½ cup salted butter, melted

Yield: 16 servings

To prepare the filling: Heat dates, coconut and half-and-half in medium saucepan over medium heat. Stir occasionally until mixture boils and thickens, about 15 minutes. Remove from heat and stir in vanilla. Set aside to cool.

To prepare the granola base: Combine oats, flour, sugar, soda and cinnamon in medium bowl. Mix well with wire whisk. Pour melted butter over dry ingredients and stir with large wooden spoon until thoroughly moistened.

Press about 3 cups of the granola mixture into bottom of an 8-by-8-inch baking pan. Place in refrigerator about 30 minutes to harden. Preheat oven to 350° F.

Spread the cooled date filling evenly over granola base. Sprinkle the remaining granola mixture (about ¾ cup) over the date filling. Bake for 25-30 minutes or until the granola topping is slightly browned and crisp. Cool to room temperature before cutting into 2-inch squares.

After the dates, coconut, and half-and-half have come to a boil continue to cook the mixture until it has thickened (left). Stir occasionally to prevent sticking.

Triple-Layered Lemon Bars

Preheat oven to 325° F.

To prepare the shortbread crust: Cream butter and sugar in medium bowl with electric mixer set on high speed. Add vanilla and mix until combined. Add flour and mix at low speed until fully incorporated. Press dough evenly into bottom of an 8-by-8-inch baking pan. Refrigerate until firm, approximately 30 minutes. Prick shortbread crust with fork and bake for 30 minutes or until crust turns golden brown. Cool on rack to room temperature.

Prepare the cream cheese filling while the crust is baking. Beat cream cheese and sugar until smooth in medium bowl with electric mixer set on high speed. Add egg and lemon extract and beat on medium speed until light and smooth. Cover bowl tightly and refrigerate.

To prepare the lemon curd: Blend the egg yolks with the cornstarch and sugar in medium non-aluminum saucepan. Place over low heat and slowly whisk in water and lemon juice. Increase heat to medium-low and cook, stirring constantly, until mixture thickens enough to coat the back of a spoon. Remove from heat. Add lemon peel and butter and cool for 10 minutes.

To assemble the bars: Spread chilled cream cheese filling evenly over cooled shortbread crust with spatula. Spread lemon curd evenly over cream cheese filling. Place pan in center of oven. Bake 30-40 minutes or until edges begin to turn light golden brown. Cool to room temperature on rack. Chill in refrigerator 1 hour before cutting into bars. Dust top with confectioners' sugar.

Crust:
½ cup salted butter, softened
¼ cup confectioners' sugar
1 tsp. pure vanilla extract
1 cup all-purpose flour

Cream Cheese Filling:
8 oz. cream cheese, softened
1½ cups confectioners' sugar
1 large egg
1 tsp. pure lemon extract

Lemon Curd:
4 large egg yolks
1 Tbsp. cornstarch
¾ cup white sugar
¾ cup water
2 medium lemons grated for 2 tsp.
lemon peel, and squeezed for ¼ cup
fresh lemon juice
2 Tbsp. salted butter, softened

Topping:
2 Tbsp. confectioners' sugar

Yield: 12 servings

Check the lemon curd to see if it has reached the desired consistency. If it thickly coats the back of a spoon, it is ready. Add the butter and lemon peel and proceed as directed above.

Chocolate Chip Butterscotch Bars

2 cups all-purpose flour
½ tsp. baking soda
1 cup dark brown sugar,
  firmly packed
1 cup salted butter, softened
1 large egg
2 tsp. pure vanilla extract
1 cup (4 oz.) chopped pecans
1½ cups (9 oz.) semisweet
  chocolate chips

Yield: 16 bars

Preheat oven to 300° F. Grease an 8-by-8-inch baking pan.

Combine flour and soda in a medium bowl. Mix well with a wire whisk. Set aside.

In a large bowl use an electric mixer to blend the sugar and butter. Add egg and vanilla, and beat at medium speed until light and smooth. Scrape down the sides of the bowl, then add the flour mixture, pecans and chocolate chips. Blend at low speed until just combined. Do not overmix.

Transfer batter into the prepared pan, and level top with a rubber spatula. Bake in center of oven for 35-45 minutes or until toothpick comes out clean but center is still soft. Cool on rack to room temperature. Cut with sharp knife into 1-by-2-inch bars.

Peanut Butter & Jelly Squares

Preheat oven to 325° F. Lightly butter a 9-by-13-inch baking pan.

In a medium bowl combine flour and baking powder. Mix well with a wire whisk and set aside.

In a medium bowl with an electric mixer on medium speed, combine butter and sugar to form a grainy paste. Add egg and vanilla, and mix until smooth. Scrape down sides of bowl. Then add flour mixture, and blend at low speed until thoroughly combined. Dough will be firm.

Divide dough into two pieces; form disks and wrap tightly in plastic wrap or a plastic bag. Refrigerate 1 hour.

On floured board using a floured rolling pin, roll out each disk to 9 by 13 inches, about ¼-inch thick. Place one piece in bottom and up the sides of baking pan. Refrigerate 10 minutes more.

Spread half the jelly on dough. Layer peanut butter on top of jelly, then top with remaining jelly. Sprinkle with confectioners' sugar. Place second dough rectangle on top of peanut-butter-and-jelly layer. Pinch down side edges all around inside of pan.

Bake 35-40 minutes or until golden brown and firm to the touch in the center. Cool in pan, then cut into squares and serve.

2½ cups all-purpose flour
½ tsp. baking powder
1 cup salted butter, softened
1 cup white sugar
1 large egg
2 tsp. pure vanilla extract
½ cup jam or jelly
¼ cup smooth peanut butter
2 Tbsp. confectioners' sugar

Yield: 24 squares

Pecan Pie Bars

Pastry:
1½ cups all-purpose flour
½ cup salted butter, chilled
5-6 Tbsp. ice water

Filling:
5 Tbsp. salted butter
1 cup dark brown sugar, firmly packed
½ cup light corn syrup
2 tsp. pure vanilla extract
3 large eggs, beaten
1½ (6 oz.) cups chopped pecans
16 pecan halves

Yield: 16 servings

Preheat oven to 350° F.

In a medium bowl combine flour and chilled butter with a pastry cutter until dough resembles coarse meal. Add water gradually and mix just until dough holds together and can be shaped into a ball. Or, use a food processor fitted with metal blade to combine flour and butter until they resemble coarse meal. Add water by tablespoonfuls and process just until a dough ball begins to form. Wrap dough tightly in plastic wrap or a plastic bag. Refrigerate 1 hour or until firm.

On floured board using a floured rolling pin, roll out dough into a 10-by-10-inch square. Fold dough in half and then into quarters. Place it in an 8-by-8-inch baking pan. Unfold the dough and press it into the corners and up along the sides of the pan. Refrigerate 15 minutes.

To prepare the filling: Melt 5 tablespoons of butter in medium saucepan over medium heat. Remove from heat, and stir in sugar and corn syrup. Mix until smooth. Add vanilla and eggs, and beat with spoon until thoroughly combined. Fold in chopped pecans.

Pour the pecan filling into the pastry-lined pan. If dough extends beyond filling mixture trim dough with a knife. Place pan in center of oven and bake 50-60 minutes or until filling is set. Cool on wire rack. Cut into 2-by-2-inch squares, and top each with a pecan half. Serve at room temperature or chilled.

To transfer the dough from the work surface to the pan, first fold it into quarters. Place the dough in the baking pan (far left), then unfold it. Press the dough into the bottom, corners, and up the sides of the pan (left). Refrigerate for 15 minutes while you prepare the filling.

Caramel-Filled Brownies

Preheat oven to 325° F. Grease an 8-by-8-inch baking pan.

In a small saucepan melt chocolate and ½ cup butter over low heat, stirring constantly. Remove from heat.

Beat eggs in a large bowl using an electric mixer set on high speed until they thicken slightly. Add sugar slowly. Add vanilla and mix well. Add chocolate-butter mixture, and beat on medium until uniformly brown. Add the flour and blend at low speed until just combined. Do not overmix.

Pour half of the brownie batter into the prepared pan. Smooth top. Bake 15-20 minutes or until top is firm.

To prepare the caramel: Heat butter, sugar and corn syrup in heavy pan over medium heat, stirring constantly until sugar dissolves. Increase heat to high and boil 1½ minutes. Remove from heat and stir in cream. Keep warm.

Spread warm caramel evenly over top of baked brownie layer. Pour remaining half of brownie mixture over caramel, smoothing the top. Bake an additional 25-30 minutes or until toothpick inserted in center comes cleanly out of top brownie layer. (Some caramel may stick to the toothpick.)

Cool brownies in pan, then cut into squares. They may be served at room temperature or chilled.

Brownies
3 oz. unsweetened chocolate
½ cup salted butter, softened
4 large eggs
1½ cups white sugar
1 Tbsp. pure vanilla extract
1½ cups all-purpose flour

Caramel:
¼ cup salted butter
⅓ cup dark brown sugar, firmly packed
2 Tbsp. light corn syrup
1 Tbsp. whipping cream

Yield: 16 servings

Vermont Maple Walnut Bars

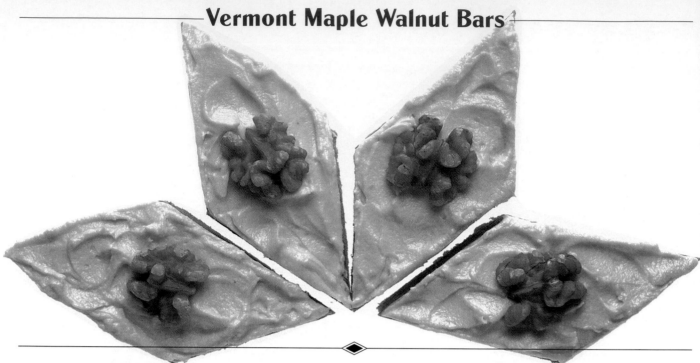

Bars:
2 cups all-purpose flour
½ tsp. baking soda
½ cup light brown sugar, packed
½ cup salted butter, softened
1 cup pure maple syrup
1 large egg
2 tsp. pure vanilla extract
1 cup (4 oz.) walnuts, chopped

Maple Frosting:
½ cup salted butter, softened
2 oz. cream cheese, softened
1 Tbsp. light brown sugar, packed
3 Tbsp. pure maple syrup
¼ cup + 2 Tbsp. confectioners' sugar
Walnut halves (optional)

Yield: 12-16 bars

Preheat oven to 325° F. Grease an 8-by-8-inch baking pan.

To make bars: In a medium bowl combine flour and soda. Mix well with a wire whisk and set aside.

In a large bowl with an electric mixer blend sugar and butter to form a grainy paste. Scrape down sides of bowl, then add syrup, egg and vanilla. Beat at medium speed until smooth.

Add the flour mixture and walnuts, and blend at low speed just until combined. Do not overmix.

Pour batter into baking pan and smooth top with a spatula. Bake 40-45 minutes or until toothpick inserted in center comes out clean. Cool in pan 15 minutes, then invert onto cooling rack. Cool completely before icing.

To make frosting: In a medium bowl cream butter and cream cheese with electric mixer at high speed. Add brown sugar and maple syrup, and beat until smooth. Reduce mixer speed to medium, and slowly add confectioners' sugar. Once sugar is incorporated, increase speed to high, and mix until smooth. If frosting appears thin, gradually add confectioners' sugar until frosting thickens.

Using a metal spatula, spread frosting on top and sides of maple bars. If desired, make designs on frosting or decorate with walnut halves.

Tuxedo Cookie Bars

Preheat oven to 325° F. Grease a 9-by-13-inch baking pan.

In a medium bowl combine flour and soda with a wire whisk, and set aside.

In a small saucepan melt butter and 2 cups of the semisweet chips over low heat, stirring constantly until smooth.

In a large bowl with an electric mixer at medium speed, beat chocolate mixture and sugar until smooth, about 5 minutes. Continuing to beat, add the vanilla, then the water, a tablespoon at a time. Scrape down sides of bowl. Next, add eggs one at a time, mixing well after each addition.

Gradually add the flour mixture, blending at low speed. Then add the remaining 1 cup of semisweet chips and the white chocolate chips. Blend until equally distributed throughout batter.

Spread batter into prepared baking pan. Bake 35-40 minutes or until toothpick inserted in center comes out just slightly moist.

Cool to room temperature. Cover well and refrigerate until cold. Cut into bars to serve.

1½ cups all-purpose flour
1 tsp. baking soda
½ cup salted butter
1½ cups white sugar
*3 cups (18 oz.) semisweet
chocolate chips*
1 Tbsp. pure vanilla extract
4 Tbsp. hot water
4 large eggs
1 cup (6 oz.) white chocolate chips

Yield: 18 servings

Creamy Peanut Butter Chocolate Bars

Crust:
8 medium-sized butter or chocolate chip cookies
¼ cup salted butter, melted

Chocolate Layers:
2½ cups (15 oz.) milk chocolate chips

Peanut Butter Filling:
1 ½ cups creamy peanut butter
½ cup salted butter, softened
3 cups confectioners' sugar
2 tsp. pure vanilla extract

Yield: 24-36 bars

Preheat oven to 325° F.

In food processor or blender process cookies until finely ground. Add butter and mix together completely. Press crumb mixture into bottom of 8-by-8-inch baking pan and bake 10 minutes. Cool to room temperature.

Melt chocolate in double boiler over slightly simmering water. Or microwave the chocolate, stirring every 30 seconds until completely melted. Pour half of the melted chocolate into pan and smooth evenly over crust. Place pan in refrigerator. Keep remaining chocolate warm.

To prepare the peanut butter filling, blend peanut butter and butter together until smooth using a food processor or electric mixer. Slowly beat in confectioners' sugar and then add vanilla. Beat until smooth. Spread peanut butter filling over the chilled chocolate layer. Finish by pouring remaining warm chocolate over filling and spreading smooth. Chill in refrigerator one hour or until firm. Cut into bars and serve.

Spoon the peanut butter filling over the chilled cocolate and cookie base (far left), then spread smooth. Complete the bar by pouring the melted chocolate over the peanut butter layer (left), spreading it smooth, and chilling in the refrigerator until firm.

Special Treats

Mocha Mousse Cheesecake

Crust:
1 cup (4 oz.) chocolate chip cookie crumbs
2 Tbsp. salted butter, melted

Filling:
Three 8 oz. pkgs. cream cheese, softened
½ cup white sugar
½ cup light brown sugar, packed
1 cup (8 oz.) sour cream
3 large eggs
1¼ cups (7 oz.) semisweet chocolate chips, melted
½ cup coffee, freshly brewed
1 Tbsp. pure vanilla extract

Glaze:
¾ cup (5 oz.) semisweet chocolate
¼ cup salted butter, softened

Yield: 12-16 servings

Preheat oven to 350° F.

To make the crust: Use a blender or a food processor with a metal blade to grind cookies into fine crumbs. Add butter and blend until smooth. Press crust into bottom of a 9-inch springform pan. Refrigerate while preparing mousse.

To make the filling: In a large bowl with an electric mixer, beat the cream cheese until very smooth. Add sugars and sour cream, and blend thoroughly. Add eggs, and beat until mixture is smooth.

Add melted chocolate, coffee and vanilla, again blending ingredients until smooth. Pour filling into prepared pan, and bake in middle of oven for 50-60 minutes.

Turn off oven, crack door 1 inch, and leave cheesecake in oven 1 hour to set. Then remove from oven and cool to room temperature.

To make the glaze: In a small saucepan melt chocolate and butter over low heat; stir until smooth. Pour glaze over top of cheesecake and smooth with a metal spatula. Refrigerate 3-4 hours or until firm. Cut and serve.

When baked cheesecake has cooled, pour chocolate-butter glaze over the top, and smooth with a metal spatula to form a thin chocolate frosting.

Chocolate Chip Cheesecake

Preheat oven to 350° F.

To prepare the crust: Grind cookies into fine crumbs using a blender or a food processor fitted with a metal blade. Add butter and blend until smooth. Press crust into bottom of 9-inch springform pan, and refrigerate while preparing the filling.

To prepare the filling: Beat cream cheese until smooth in a large bowl using an electric mixer. Blend in sugar and sour cream. Add the eggs and vanilla, and mix until smooth.

Using a wooden spoon, stir in 1 cup of the chocolate chips. Pour filling into the crust-lined pan, and smooth top with a spatula. Sprinkle the remaining ½ cup chocolate chips evenly over the top. Bake 30-40 minutes. Turn oven off and leave cheesecake in oven for 1 hour to set. Remove from oven and chill in refrigerator until firm, about 3-4 hours.

Crust:
1 cup (5 oz.) chocolate cookie crumbs
2 Tbsp. salted butter, softened

Filling:
16 oz. cream cheese, softened
1 cup white sugar
2 cups (16 oz.) sour cream
3 large eggs
1 Tbsp. pure vanilla extract
1½ cups (9 oz.) semisweet chocolate chips, divided

Yield: 12-16 servings

Cake:
3 cups cake flour, sifted
2 cups white sugar
½ tsp. salt
1 tsp. baking powder
1½ cups salted butter, softened
⅓ cup buttermilk,
at room temperature
6 large eggs
2 tsp. pure lemon extract
1 Tbsp. grated lemon zest
(2 medium lemons)

Glaze:
¼ cup freshly squeezed lemon juice
¼ cup white sugar

Topping:
2 Tbsp. confectioners' sugar, sifted

Yield: 2 dozen slices

Preheat oven to 350° F. Grease and flour a 3-quart fluted tube pan or bundt pan.

In a large bowl with an electric mixer on low speed, blend flour, sugar, salt and baking powder. Add butter, buttermilk and 3 eggs. Beat on low until dry ingredients are moistened. Increase speed to high and beat for 2 minutes. Scrape down sides of bowl.

Add lemon extract and lemon zest, and blend at medium speed. Add the remaining 3 eggs one at a time, beating at high speed for 30 seconds after each addition.

Pour batter into prepared pan, and bake 50-60 minutes or until a toothpick inserted into cake comes out clean.

While pound cake is baking, prepare lemon glaze. In a small saucepan heat lemon juice and sugar over low heat. Stir constantly until sugar dissolves.

When cake is done, remove from oven and leave cake in pan. With a toothpick, poke holes in the surface of the cake, and pour half the glaze over it.

Cool in pan 15 minutes, then invert on cooling rack. Brush top of pound cake with remaining lemon glaze. Cool to room temperature, then dust with confectioners' sugar.

With a toothpick, poke holes in the surface of the cake (far left). Then pour the lemon glaze over the holes, letting it drizzle into the cake (left). Saturating this pound cake with lemon is the secret to its moistness.

Poppy-Seed Bundt Cake

Preheat oven to 350° F. Grease and flour a 3-quart fluted tube pan or bundt pan.

In large bowl with an electric mixer blend flour, sugar, salt and baking powder on low until all ingredients are distributed equally. Add butter, sour cream and 3 of the eggs, and mix on medium until the dry ingredients are moistened. Beat on high for 2 minutes, then scrape bowl.

Add remaining 3 eggs, one at a time, alternating with the sherry. Beat well after each addition. Blend in poppy seeds on low speed.

Pour batter into prepared pan and bake 50-60 minutes or until toothpick inserted into the center of cake comes out clean. Cool in pan 10 minutes, then invert cake onto a rack to cool. When cake has cooled completely, lightly dust top with confectioners' sugar.

3 cups cake flour, sifted
2 cups white sugar
½ tsp. salt
1 tsp. baking powder
1½ cups salted butter, softened
½ cup (4 oz.) sour cream
6 large eggs
⅓ cup cream sherry
⅓ cup poppy seeds

Topping:
¼ cup confectioners' sugar

Yield: 24 servings

Classic Apple Pie

Crust:
3 cups all-purpose flour
2 tsp. grated lemon zest
(1 medium lemon)
1 cup salted butter, chilled
6-8 Tbsp. ice water

Filling:
6 large Granny Smith apples, peeled
and thinly sliced (about 4 cups)
1 cup white sugar
1 tsp. ground cinnamon
¼ cup cornstarch
¼ cup salted butter, chilled and cut
into small pieces

Egg Wash:
1 large egg, beaten
1 Tbsp. white sugar

Yield: 8 slices

To prepare crust: Mix flour and lemon zest together with wire whisk in a medium bowl. With pastry cutter or 2 knives, cut in butter with flour until dough resembles coarse meal.

Add ice water and blend until dough can be gathered into a ball. Divide dough in half, flatten into disks, and wrap tightly in plastic wrap or a plastic bag. Refrigerate 1 hour or until firm.

To prepare filling: Combine sugar, cinnamon and cornstarch with a wire whisk in a large bowl. Add apples to sugar mixture and toss with a wooden spoon until dry ingredients coat the apples completely.

Preheat oven to 400° F.

On a floured surface use a floured rolling pin to roll out one piece of dough into a circle 11 inches in diameter. Fold the crust in half, then in quarters.

Place point of folded crust in center of a 9-inch pie plate and carefully unfold. Trim excess dough, leaving about ¾ inch hanging over edge of plate.

Spoon in apple filling and sprinkle butter pieces on top.

To prepare top crust: Roll out second piece of dough into a circle 10 inches in diameter. Again, fold in half, then quarters, and place on top of filling. Fold extra crust of the top layer over the bottom layer. Crimp layers together decoratively.

Cut several steam slits in pie top, brush with egg wash, and sprinkle with 1 tablespoon sugar.

Place pie on center rack of oven. Bake for 20 minutes, then reduce heat to 350° F. Bake an additional 30 minutes, or until crust is deep golden brown and filling is bubbling through steam slits.

Remove from oven and cool to room temperature on rack.

After spooning in the apple filling, cover pie with the top crust. Trim excess dough with a paring knife, leaving about ¾ inch hanging over (above). Fold the extra crust of the top layer over the bottom layer and crimp layers together decoratively (right). Before baking, cut small vent holes in the top crust to allow steam to escape (far right).

Super Fudge Brownies

6 oz. unsweetened baking chocolate
1 cup salted butter, softened
4 large eggs
2 cups white sugar
1 Tbsp. pure vanilla extract
½ cup all-purpose flour
1 cup (6 oz.) semisweet
chocolate chips

Yield: 16 brownies, 2 inches square

Preheat oven to 300° F. Grease an 8-by-8-inch baking pan.

Combine unsweetened baking chocolate and butter in a medium saucepan. Melt over medium-low heat, stirring constantly until pieces are almost melted. Remove from heat and stir until smooth.

In a large bowl, using an electric mixer on medium speed, beat eggs until light yellow in color—about 5 minutes. Add sugar and blend on low until thoroughly combined.

Add vanilla and melted chocolate to the egg and sugar mixture. Blend on low speed until smooth. Add the flour and mix thoroughly.

Pour batter into greased pan. Smooth surface with a spatula, and sprinkle uniformly with chocolate chips. Bake on the center rack of oven for 45-55 minutes. The batter should be set and a toothpick inserted in center should come out clean. Do not overbake.

Cool to room temperature. Cover and refrigerate for at least 1 hour. Cut and serve chilled.

Chocolate Pecan Tartlets

To prepare pastry: In medium bowl combine flour and butter with pastry cutter until dough resembles coarse meal. Add egg yolks and water, then mix with a fork just until dough can be shaped into a ball.

Gather dough into a ball. Wrap tightly in plastic wrap or a plastic bag. Refrigerate until firm—about 1 hour.

To prepare filling: In a 2-quart saucepan combine butter and chocolate, stirring constantly over low heat. Transfer to medium bowl and let cool for 5 minutes. With an electric mixer on medium speed, beat eggs into chocolate mixture. Add sugar, corn syrup and vanilla, and blend on low speed until smooth. Fold in pecans.

Preheat oven to 350° F.

To assemble tartlets: On lightly floured counter or board, use a lightly floured rolling pin to roll out dough to ⅛-inch thickness. Using a 2½-inch fluted tartlet pan as a guide, cut dough ¼ inch around entire edge. Repeat with remaining dough. Lay dough rounds in tartlet pans and press in firmly.

Fill pans two-thirds full of chocolate pecan filling. Place on baking sheet to catch any drips. Bake for 30-35 minutes, or until filling is set and does not look wet.

While still warm, place one pecan half in center of each tartlet. Meanwhile, chill mixing bowl and beaters in freezer.

To prepare topping: In a medium bowl with electric mixer set on high, beat cream, sugar and vanilla until stiff peaks form. Do not overbeat. Transfer the whipped topping to a pastry bag fitted with a medium star tip, and pipe decorative topping onto each tartlet.

With a paring knife, cut rolled dough around edge of inverted tartlet pan, leaving ¼-inch excess, as shown in inset. Repeat with remaining dough. Then press dough rounds firmly into tartlet pans (right).

Pastry:
2 cups all-purpose flour
1 cup salted butter
2 large egg yolks
2-3 Tbsp. ice water

Filling:
½ cup salted butter
4 oz. unsweetened baking chocolate
2 large eggs
1 cup dark brown sugar, packed
½ cup corn syrup
2 tsp. pure vanilla extract
1½ cups pecans, chopped

Topping:
24 pecan halves
½ cup heavy cream
¼ cup white sugar
1 tsp. pure vanilla extract

Yield: 24 2½-inch tartlets

Chocolate Meringue Puffs

2 oz. unsweetened baking chocolate
¾ cup confectioners' sugar, sifted
3 Tbsp. unsweetened
cocoa powder, sifted
3 large egg whites
½ tsp. cream of tartar
½ cup white sugar

Yield: 2½ dozen

Line baking sheets with foil.

Finely chop baking chocolate square in a blender, and set aside.

In a small bowl combine confectioners' sugar and cocoa with wire whisk.

In a medium bowl beat egg whites and cream of tartar with an electric mixer at medium speed until mixture thickens. Increase speed to high, while adding sugar slowly. Beat until mixture forms stiff peaks and turns glossy.

Gently fold in cocoa mixture and chopped baking chocolate with a rubber spatula. Fold ingredients into egg whites until mixture is uniformly brown with no streaks.

Fill a pastry bag fitted with a large star tip with the meringue. Pipe meringue in decorative shapes onto foil-lined baking sheets.

Preheat oven to 200° F.

Allow meringues to dry at room temperature for about 45 minutes or until not sticky. (Don't try making these on humid or rainy days.) Bake for 1 hour. When cool, remove from foil with a metal spatula.

Spoon the meringue into a pastry bag with a large star tip. Pipe meringue in decorative shapes onto foil-lined baking sheets. If you don't have a pastry bag, drop the meringue by tablespoonfuls onto the foil.

Bread Pudding

Preheat oven to 325° F. Butter sides and bottom of 9-by-13-inch baking pan.

Butter one side of each bread slice and layer in pan alternately with croissants (6 slices bread, croissant slices, 6 slices bread).

In large bowl with an electric mixer set on medium-high speed beat eggs until slightly thickened, about 5 minutes. Add sugar and vanilla and beat at medium speed until thoroughly combined. Reduce speed to low and add cream; mix until smooth.

Pour egg-cream mixture over bread and croissant slices. The slices will absorb egg-cream mixture slowly, so continue adding liquid until all is in pan.

In small bowl combine cinnamon, nutmeg and ⅛ teaspoon sugar. Sprinkle sugar-spice mixture over the bread pudding.

Fill a baking pan larger than the 9-by-13-inch bread pudding pan halfway up with hot water. Place in oven. Set bread pudding pan in the water bath. Bake 45-50 minutes or until custard is set. When set, remove bread pudding from the oven, and discard water in larger pan. Cool to room temperature. Refrigerate for 2 hours or until firm.

12 slices raisin nut bread
½ cup salted butter, room temperature
2 butter croissants, sliced lengthwise into ¼-inch slices
6 large eggs
1 cup plus ⅛ tsp. white sugar, divided
1 Tbsp. pure vanilla extract
4 cups (1 quart) light cream or half-and-half
½ tsp. ground cinnamon
⅛ tsp. ground nutmeg

Yield: 12 servings

Carrot Cake

Cake:
2½ cups all-purpose flour
2 tsp. baking soda
¼ tsp. salt
2 tsp. cinnamon
1 cup light brown sugar, packed
1 cup white sugar
1½ cups salted butter, softened
3 large eggs
2 tsp. pure vanilla extract
3 cups grated carrot
(3 to 4 medium carrots)
½ cup crushed pineapple, drained
1 cup (6 oz.) raisins
1 cup (4 oz.) chopped walnuts

Icing:
16 oz. cream cheese, softened
½ cup salted butter, softened
1 Tbsp. fresh lemon juice (about 1 large lemon)
2 tsp. pure vanilla extract
3 cups confectioners' sugar

Yield: 12-16 servings

With a metal spatula, spread icing over bottom cake layer to form a thin filling (right). Top with second cake layer, and ice the surface and sides evenly. For an elegant finish, pipe on a border with a pastry bag and a medium star tip (far right).

Preheat oven to 350° F. Grease and flour two 9-inch cake pans.

In a large bowl stir together flour, baking soda, salt, cinnamon and sugars. Add butter, one egg and vanilla; blend with electric mixer on low speed. Increase speed to medium and beat for 2 minutes.

Scrape down sides of bowl. Add remaining eggs, one at a time, beating 30 seconds after each addition. Add carrots, pineapple, raisins and walnuts. Blend on low until thoroughly combined.

Pour batter into prepared pans and smooth the surface with a rubber spatula. Bake in center of oven for 60-70 minutes. Toothpick inserted into center should come out clean. Cool in pans for 10 minutes. Then invert cakes on rack and cool to room temperature.

To prepare icing: On a medium bowl with electric mixer on medium speed, beat cream cheese and butter until smooth. Add lemon juice and vanilla; beat until combined. Add sugar gradually, mixing on low until smooth.

To ice the carrot cake: Place one layer on a cake platter, and with a metal spatula spread icing over the top to form a thin filling. Place second layer over the first, rounded side up. Coat the top and sides of the cake evenly with remaining icing. Refrigerate 1 hour to set icing.

Chocolate Waffle Pillows

Grease and preheat waffle iron.

In medium bowl combine flour, baking powder and cocoa. Mix well with a wire whisk. Set aside.

In large bowl with an electric mixer cream butter and sugar. Add eggs and vanilla and beat at medium speed. Batter will appear slightly curdled. Scrape down the sides of the bowl, then add the flour mixture and blend on low speed until just combined. Do not overmix.

Drop by rounded tablespoons onto hot waffle iron, using about one tablespoon per 4-by-4-inch square. Cook approximately 1 minute. Carefully transfer to cool surface.

Use any of the following toppings singly or in combination: a dusting of confectioners' sugar and cocoa powder; fresh raspberries and whipped cream; a drizzle of chocolate syrup.

Waffles:
2 cups all-purpose flour
1 tsp. baking powder
1 cup unsweetened cocoa powder
1 cup salted butter, softened
2 cups white sugar
5 large eggs
2 tsp. pure vanilla extract

Toppings:
⅓ cup confectioners' sugar
⅓ cup unsweetened cocoa powder
1 cup fresh raspberries
1 pint whipping cream, whipped
½ cup chocolate syrup

Yield: 3½ dozen

Chocolate Macadamia Cream Satin

Cake:
1 cup all-purpose flour
1½ tsp. baking soda
1 tsp. salt
¾ cup light brown sugar, packed
¾ cup white sugar
½ cup salted butter, softened
¼ cup unsweetened cocoa powder
¼ cup boiling water
2 large eggs, beaten
1 tsp. pure vanilla extract
1 cup buttermilk

Filling:
¼ cup white sugar
14 oz. cream cheese, at room temperature
1 large egg
1 lb. white chocolate bar
2½ tsp. (1 pkg.) unflavored gelatin
2 Tbsp. cold water
1 cup (½ pint) whipping cream
3 Tbsp. pure vanilla extract

Decorations:
4 cups (24 oz.) unsalted macadamia nuts
¼ cup cocoa powder
¼ cup confectioners' sugar
½ cup (¼ pint) whipping cream (optional)
1 oz. dark or white chocolate (optional)

Yield: 12 servings

Preheat oven to 350° F. Grease and flour an 8- or 9-inch springform pan.

In medium bowl combine flour, baking soda and salt. Mix well with a wire whisk and set aside.

In large bowl combine sugars with an electric mixer on medium speed. Add butter and beat to form a grainy paste.

In small bowl combine cocoa powder and boiling water, and stir until smooth. Add cocoa mixture, eggs and vanilla to butter and sugar; blend well to form a smooth batter. Alternately add the flour mixture and the buttermilk to the batter. Blend at low speed just until combined.

Pour into prepared pan. Bake 25-35 minutes or until a knife inserted into middle of the cake comes out clean. Leaving cake in pan, cool to room temperature, then refrigerate to make slicing easier.

To prepare the filling: In medium bowl with an electric mixer and clean beaters, beat sugar and cream cheese until well blended. Add egg and beat until light and fluffy.

Next melt white chocolate in a double boiler. While chocolate is melting, in a small metal bowl sprinkle gelatin over the cold water. Let gelatin bloom for 5 minutes, then dissolve it over a double boiler until clear and smooth.

Gradually add dissolved gelatin to the cream cheese-sugar mixture, beating continuously at medium speed until smooth. (If you beat it too fast, the gelatin will stick to the sides of the bowl.)

Add whipped cream to the mixture and blend until smooth. With a rubber spatula, fold the white chocolate and vanilla into the cake batter thoroughly.

To assemble cake and filling: Remove sides of springform pan. Cut cake into 2 thin layers and set the top layer aside. Replace sides of the springform pan, leaving bottom layer of cake in pan.

Pour filling over bottom cake layer. Carefully place the other cake layer on top of the filling. Refrigerate for several hours.

When filling is firm, remove sides of pan and place the cake on a platter. Coat the sides of the cake with macadamia nuts. Dust the top of the cake with a mixture of cocoa powder and confectioners' sugar. If desired, add rosettes of whipped cream, chocolate shavings and more macadamia nuts. Refrigerate until ready to serve.

Using a bread knife, carefully cut cake into two thin layers (top). Return bottom layer to springform pan, and pour the filling on top (right). Finally, cap the filling with the top cake layer (far right).

Coffee Toffee Chocolate Crunch

6 Tbsp. salted butter
1 cup white sugar
¼ cup water
2 tsp. coffee liqueur
¼ tsp. baking soda
½ cup (3 oz.) semisweet
chocolate chips

Lightly grease a 9-by-13-inch glass baking dish.

In a heavy 2-quart saucepan, combine butter, sugar and water. Heat over medium temperature, stirring with a wooden spoon until sugar dissolves. Cover pan for 2 minutes to wash down any sugar crystals.

Uncover pan and increase heat to high. Without stirring, continue cooking until mixture begins to turn golden brown.

Quickly remove from heat; stir in coffee liqueur and baking soda. Pour immediately into prepared baking dish. Spread thin with a wooden spoon. Cool to room temperature.

In a small saucepan, melt chocolate chips, stirring constantly until smooth. Then, dip a fork into the chocolate and drizzle lattice patterns over the toffee candy. Let stand until chocolate is set. Break toffee into irregular-sized pieces. Store in an airtight container.

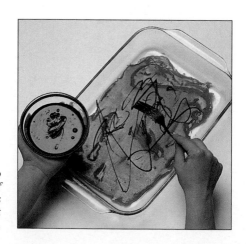

To decorate the cooled toffee, dip a fork into melted chocolate. Let the chocolate drizzle off the tines onto the candy in interesting swirls and lattice patterns. Allow chocolate to set before breaking the candy into bite-sized pieces.

Macadamia Nut Brittle

Lightly grease a 9-by-13-inch glass baking dish. Equally distribute macadamia nuts over bottom of dish. Set aside.

In a heavy 2-quart saucepan, combine butter, sugar and water. Place over medium heat and stir with a wooden spoon until sugar dissolves. Let pan stand covered for 2 minutes.

Uncover pan and increase heat to high. Continue cooking without stirring until mixture begins to turn golden brown. Quickly remove from heat; stir in baking soda and vanilla extract. Pour immediately over macadamia nuts in prepared baking dish. Spread with a wooden spoon.

Cool to room temperature. Break into irregular-sized pieces. Store in an airtight container.

*1½ cups (9 oz.) whole macadamia
nuts
6 Tbsp. salted butter
1 cup white sugar
¼ cup water
¼ tsp. baking soda
1 tsp. pure vanilla extract*

Yield: About 1 pound of brittle

Heat the butter-sugar combination over high heat until it turns a rich, golden brown, as shown at far left. Immediately pour the liquid over the macadamia nuts. Use a wooden spoon to distribute the nuts evenly around the pan (left). Allow the brittle to cool before breaking into bite-sized pieces.

Chocolate Custard-Filled Meringues

Custard:
*1½ cups light cream
one 1½-inch piece vanilla bean split
in half lengthwise
(or 2 tsp. pure vanilla extract)
4 large egg yolks
2 Tbsp. cornstarch
½ cup white sugar
1 cup (6 oz.) semisweet
chocolate chips*

Meringue:
*3 large egg whites
½ tsp. cream of tartar
⅓ cup white sugar
½ tsp. pure vanilla extract*

Yield: 3 dozen

To make the chocolate custard: In a medium saucepan scald cream with vanilla bean.

In a small bowl lightly beat egg yolks with cornstarch until no lumps remain. Add sugar, then slowly whisk in 1 cup of the hot cream. Pour yolk-cream mixture back into the saucepan and cook over medium-low heat, stirring constantly until mixture thickens enough to coat the back of a spoon. Do not boil or the egg will curdle.

Transfer custard into a medium bowl, and stir in chocolate chips until melted. If you are using vanilla extract, stir it in with the chocolate chips.

To make the meringue: In a medium bowl with an electric mixer on high speed, beat egg whites until foamy. Add cream of tartar and half of the sugar; continue mixing until thickened—about 5 minutes. While still beating, add the remaining sugar slowly until stiff peaks form. Finally, beat in the vanilla. Do not overbeat or peaks may fall.

Transfer meringue to pastry bag with a large plain tip. Pipe 1-inch balls onto lightly greased and foil-lined baking sheets. (Too much butter on the sheets will cause meringues to slide.) If you don't have a pastry bag, drop meringue by rounded teaspoonfuls.

With index finger coated in flour, poke holes in center of each meringue, about ½ inch in diameter. This will hold the custard after the meringues are baked.

Preheat oven to 225° F. Set meringues out to dry for 45 minutes. Then bake for 35-45 minutes, just until meringue turns golden brown.

Cool meringues to room temperature. With pastry bag or small spoon, fill meringues with chocolate custard.

*Slowly add sugar to the thickened egg whites
(far left), and beat until stiff peaks form.
Continuous beating gives the meringue the air
it needs to stand up (left), but overbeating
may cause it to fall.*

Caramel Chocolate Tartlets

In medium bowl combine flour, sugar and butter with a pastry cutter until dough resembles coarse meal. Add egg yolks, vanilla. Gradually add ice water until dough can be shaped into a ball. Or, use a food processor fitted with a metal blade to combine flour, sugar and butter until dough resembles coarse meal. Add egg yolks, vanilla and ice water by tablespoonfuls, and process until dough begins to form a ball.

Flatten dough into a disk and wrap tightly in plastic wrap or place in plastic bag. Chill 1 hour or until firm.

On floured board using a floured rolling pin, roll out dough to ¼ inch thickness. Cut 4-inch rounds to fit into 3½-inch-diameter tart pans. Gently press into tart pans and place in refrigerator for 15 minutes. Preheat oven to 400° F.

Remove tart shells from refrigerator and prick bottoms with a fork. Bake 13-15 minutes or until edges begin to turn golden brown. Cool tart shells to room temperature.

To prepare the caramel filling: Combine butter, brown sugar and corn syrup in a heavy 2-quart saucepan. Place over medium heat, and stir constantly until sugar dissolves. Turn heat to high and boil without stirring for 2 minutes, or until large bubbles form.

Remove from heat and stir in cream. Cool caramel 5 minutes and then pour into tart shells. Cool caramel tartlets to room temperature. Use a vegetable peeler to slowly and carefully shave curls from the chocolate bar. Sprinkle tartlets with chocolate curls.

Pastry:
1½ cups all-purpose flour
¼ cup white sugar
½ cup salted butter, chilled
2 large egg yolks
1 tsp. pure vanilla extract
4-5 Tbsp. ice water

Caramel Filling:
¾ cup salted butter
1 cup dark brown sugar,
firmly packed
⅓ cup light corn syrup
3 tbsp. heavy cream
one 16-oz. solid semisweet or milk
chocolate bar, room temperature

Yield: 8 tartlets

As you press the 4-inch rounds into the tart pans, press the excess dough off the top edge (top). Chill the lined pans for 15 minutes, then use a fork to prick holes in the bottom of each crust (inset)—this will keep the bottom from ballooning up during baking.

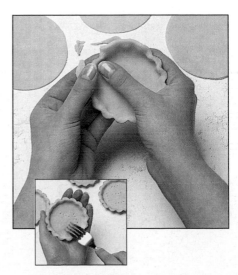

109

Brownies Espresso

Brownies:
2½ cups all-purpose flour
½ tsp. baking soda
1 cup dark brown sugar, packed
½ cup white sugar
1 cup salted butter, softened
2 oz. unsweetened baking chocolate
1 Tbsp. instant espresso or instant
coffee granules
1 Tbsp. boiling water
2 large eggs
1 tsp. pure vanilla extract
1 tsp. pure almond extract
1 cup (6 oz.) semisweet
chocolate chips

Glaze:
3 oz. semisweet chocolate
⅓ cup salted butter, softened
½ cup sliced almonds

Yield: 12-16 servings

Preheat oven to 325° F. Grease an 8-by-8-inch baking pan.

In a medium bowl combine flour and soda. Mix well with a wire whisk and set aside.

In a large bowl blend sugars with an electric mixer at medium speed. Add butter and mix to form a grainy paste.

Melt baking chocolate in a double boiler. Meanwhile, in a small bowl, dissolve espresso or coffee granules in boiling water.

Add chocolate and coffee to sugar and butter; beat at medium speed until smooth. Add eggs, vanilla and extracts; beat until smooth.

Scrape down sides of bowl. Add the flour mixture and chocolate chips, and blend at low speed just until combined. Do not overmix.

Pour batter into greased baking pan. Bake 35-40 minutes or until toothpick placed in center comes out clean. Cool in pan 15 minutes. Invert on rack.

To make glaze: Melt together the chocolate and butter in a double boiler, stirring until smooth.

Spread glaze over brownies and sprinkle with almonds. Cool completely before cutting into bars.

Chocolate Swirl Banana Cake

Preheat oven to 350° F. Grease an 8-by-8-inch baking pan.

In medium bowl combine flour and soda. Mix well with a wire whisk. Set aside.

Blend sugar and butter in a large bowl using an electric mixer. Scrape sides of bowl. Add sour cream, banana, egg and vanilla, and beat at medium speed until smooth. Add the flour mixture and blend at low speed until just combined. Do not overmix. Gently fold in melted chocolate and stir just until marbled pattern develops.

Pour batter into the prepared pan. Bake 40-45 minutes or until toothpick inserted into center comes out clean. Cool in pan 15 minutes, then invert onto rack and cool to room temperature.

To prepare the ganache: Scald cream in a small saucepan. Remove from heat and add chocolate. Cover pan with lid and set aside. After about 15 minutes, stir frosting until it is smooth. Transfer to bowl and refrigerate until firm, about 30 minutes. Turn cake right side up onto a serving plate and frost liberally with the ganache.

2¼ cups all-purpose flour
1 tsp. baking soda
1¼ cups light brown sugar,
firmly packed
¼ cup salted butter
½ cup sour cream
1½ cups mashed banana
(about 3 large bananas)
1 large egg
1 tsp. pure vanilla extract
¾ cup (4½ oz.) semisweet chocolate
chips, melted

Ganache:
½ cup heavy cream
⅔ cup (4 oz.) semisweet chocolate,
finely chopped

Yield: 16 servings

Pour the melted chocolate directly into the cake batter (far left). Stir the chocolate into the batter only until a swirled, marbled pattern forms (left). The cake will show the swirl when baked.

111

Creamy Chocolate Fantasy

Pastry:
1½ cups all purpose flour
2 Tbsp. white sugar
½ cup salted butter, chilled and cut
into 8 pieces
5-6 Tbsp. ice water

Custard Filling:
1½ cups light cream
One 1½-inch vanilla bean split in
half lengthwise or
2 tsp. pure vanilla extract
4 large egg yolks
½ cup white sugar
2 Tbsp. corn starch
1 cup (6 oz.) semisweet
chocolate chips

Meringue:
3 large egg whites
½ tsp. cream of tartar
⅓ cup confectioners' sugar

Yield: 3 dozen tartlets

To make pastry: In a medium bowl combine flour, sugar and butter with a pastry cutter until dough resembles coarse meal. Add water, and mix with a fork just until dough can be shaped into a ball.

Wrap dough tightly in plastic wrap or a plastic bag. Refrigerate 1 hour or until firm.

To make custard filling: In a medium saucepan scald cream with vanilla bean.

In a small bowl lightly beat yolks with cornstarch until no lumps remain. Add sugar, then slowly whisk in 1 cup of the hot Pour yolk-cream back into the saucepan, and cook over me heat, stirring constantly until mixture thickens enough to co k of a spoon. Do not boil or egg will curdle.

Transfer custard into a medium bowl, and stir in hips until melted. If you're using vanilla extract, stir it in with the chocolate chips. Wrap custard tightly and refrigerate.

To make meringue: In a medium bowl with an electric mixer on high speed, beat egg whites until foamy. Add cream of tartar and half the sugar; beat until thickened. Gradually add the remaining sugar, beating continuously on high just until stiff peaks form. Do not overbeat or peaks may fall.

Preheat oven to 400° F.

To assemble: On floured surface with a floured rolling pin, roll out dough to ¼-inch thickness. Use a cookie cutter or a drinking glass 2 inches in diameter to cut out rounds of dough. Lightly press pastry into miniature muffin or pastry cups.

Refrigerate 15 minutes. Then prick bottom and sides of each pastry cup with a fork. Bake 10-12 minutes or until edges turn golden brown. Cool pastry to room temperature.

Spoon (or pipe with a pastry bag) 1 tablespoon of cooled chocolate custard into each pastry cup and top with meringue.

Reduce oven temperature to 350° F. Bake pastries 6-8 minutes, or until meringue begins to turn light golden brown. Cool and serve.

Use a pastry bag with a medium plain or star tip to pipe a tablespoon of chocolate custard into each pastry cup (left). Top with a swirl of meringue, covering the custard completely (below).

Baby Banana Cream Pies

Pastry:
1½ cups all-purpose flour
2 Tbsp. white sugar
½ cup salted butter, chilled and cut into 8 pieces
1 tsp. pure vanilla extract
4-5 Tbsp. ice water

Pastry Cream:
2 cups light cream
one 1-inch piece vanilla bean, split in half lengthwise or 2 tsp. pure vanilla extract
½ cup white sugar
2 Tbsp. all-purpose flour
4 large egg yolks, lightly beaten
2 Tbsp. salted butter
1 tsp. crème de banana liqueur or 1 tsp. pure banana extract

Topping:
1 cup heavy cream
¼ cup confectioners' sugar
½ tsp. pure vanilla extract
2 large or 3 medium bananas, cut into thin slices

Yield: 12 baby banana pies

To prepare the pastry: In medium bowl combine flour, sugar and butter with a pastry cutter until dough resembles coarse meal. Add water and vanilla with fork and mix until dough can be shaped into a ball. Or use a food processor fitted with metal blade to combine flour, sugar and butter until dough resembles coarse meal. Add vanilla and water gradually and process just until a ball forms. Tightly wrap dough in plastic wrap or plastic bag and place in refrigerator 1 hour or until firm.

To prepare the pastry cream: Scald cream with vanilla bean in heavy saucepan set over medium heat. Remove from heat. In small bowl whisk together the sugar and flour. Slowly pour the sugar-flour mixture into the hot cream, whisking constantly. Place saucepan back over medium heat, stirring constantly until mixture thickens enough to coat the back of a spoon.

Temper egg yolks by pouring 1 cup of hot cream mixture into yolks, stirring briskly. Pour warmed egg mixture into saucepan and continue cooking over medium heat. Stir constantly until mixture thickens enough to coat the back of a spoon. Do not boil.

Remove from heat and transfer filling to bowl. If using vanilla extract, stir it in along with the butter and banana liqueur. Cover with plastic wrap and chill thoroughly in refrigerator.

Preheat oven to 400° F.

On floured board using a floured rolling pin, roll out dough to ⅛ inch thickness. Cut out 4-inch rounds and press into bottoms and up sides of muffin tin. Reuse dough scraps until all cups have been lined. Chill dough in refrigerator 15 minutes.

Prick dough on bottom and sides with fork. Bake 15 minutes or until pastry begins to turn golden brown. Remove from oven and cool to room temperature.

To prepare the whipped cream: Beat cream with confectioners' sugar and vanilla with an electric mixer set on high speed until stiff peaks form.

Assemble the pies by placing 2 thin banana slices in bottom of each pastry shell. Top with pastry cream, add more banana slices and top with whipped cream. Serve immediately.

Cut 4-inch rounds out of the pastry dough (above). Press the rounds into the cups of a medium- to large-sized muffin tin (right). Repeat the procedure until you have lined 12 cups. Prick the sides and bottom of the dough with a fork, then bake as directed.

Banana Nut Bread

2½ cups all-purpose flour
1½ tsp. baking soda
½ tsp. salt
¾ cup salted butter, softened
1 ½ cups light brown sugar, packed
2 large eggs
3 cups ripe bananas
(about 7 medium), mashed
1 tsp. pure vanilla extract
1 cup (4 oz.) chopped walnuts

Yield: 30 ½-inch slices
(15 slices per loaf)

Preheat oven to 325° F. Grease two 9-by-5-inch loaf pans.

In a medium bowl combine flour, soda and salt with a wire whisk; set aside.

In a large bowl cream butter and sugar with an electric mixer. Add eggs, bananas and vanilla, and beat at medium speed until thick. Scrape down sides of bowl.

Add the flour mixture and walnuts, then blend at low speed just until combined. Do not overmix.

Pour batter into prepared pans. Bake on center rack of oven for 60-70 minutes. A toothpick inserted in center should come out clean, and the bread should pull away from the sides.

Cool in pan, for 10 minutes. Turn pans on sides; cool to room temperature before removing and slicing.

Mrs. Fields Macadamia Nut Tart

To prepare the crust: Combine flour, sugar and butter, and work with a pastry cutter until dough resembles coarse meal. Add egg yolks and water, and mix with a fork just until dough can be shaped into a ball. Or, using a food processor fitted with a metal blade, combine flour, sugar and butter. Process until dough resembles coarse meal. Add egg yolks and water and process just until a ball begins to form.

Shape dough into a disk and wrap tightly in plastic wrap or plastic bag. Chill in refrigerator 1 hour or until firm.

To prepare the filling: Combine the corn syrup, butter, sugar, molasses and salt in a double boiler. Bring to a boil over medium heat, stirring occasionally. Remove from heat and cool to room temperature. Once cool, add the eggs and vanilla and stir until smooth. Set syrup mixture aside until ready to use. (Mixture can be made up to two days in advance and refrigerated until ready to use.)

To assemble the tart: Preheat oven to 300° F. Spray vegetable-oil cooking spray on an 8- or 9-inch tart pan with a removable bottom.

On a floured board using a floured rolling pin, roll out dough to a 10-inch circle, ¼ inch thick. Place pastry in pan, lightly pressing it into the bottom and sides. Roll off excess dough from the top edge with rolling pin.

Fill the pastry shell with the macadamia nuts. Pour filling over nuts, and bake 90 minutes or until golden brown. Let pie cool, remove sides of pan, and serve. Garnish with whipped cream, if desired.

Pastry Crust:
1¾ cups all-purpose flour
¼ cup white sugar
½ cup salted butter, chilled
2 large egg yolks
3 Tbsp. ice water

Filling:
1 cup corn syrup
½ cup plus 3 Tbsp. salted butter
1 cup white sugar
2 Tbsp. unsulfured molasses
¼ tsp. salt
2 large eggs, lightly beaten
1 tsp. pure vanilla extract
2½ cups unsalted dry-roasted macadamia nuts
whipped cream (optional)

Yield: 12 servings

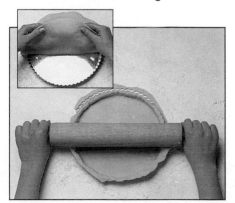

Fold the dough in half then drape it over the prepared tart pan (right, top). Gently press the dough into the pan. Be sure that there is enough dough pressed into the fluted edges to support the filling when baked. Use a rolling pin to roll off the excess dough (right).

Index

Acknowledgments

The author and editors would like to thank the following people for their assistance in the preparation of this volume:

San Francisco, California: Gay Winterringer; **Washington, D.C.:** Jody Boozel, Henry Grossi, Haas Heart, Kelly Kalibat, Kitchen Bazaar; **Park City, Utah:** Chuck and Sheila Borash, Tracy Brower, Janet Bushnell, Ed Clissold, Mary Coleman, Christy Fowers, Shelley Francis, Karen Gilmartin, Larry Holman, Shirley James, Jackie Manuell, Brett Markowski, June Ann Oldham, E.G. Perry, Tara Prescott, Janet Rees, Lisa Richards, Karrie Lynn Simmons, Jean Slusher, Ruby Stokes, Doree Tateoka, Keith Vreeken, and Lavita Wai; *special thanks to* Michael Lunter; *extra special thanks to* Jessica, Jenessa, Jennifer, Ashley, and McKenzie Fields; **Alexandria, Virginia:** Dana Coleman, Phyllis Gardner, Becky Merson, Terry Paredes, Gary Stoiber, and Becky Wheeler. The index was prepared by Barbara L. Klein, Cheyenne, Wyoming. Additional photography on p. 5 and back cover by Zeke McCabe Photography, Salt Lake City, Utah.

For further information about the recipes in this book, please write to:
   c/o Customer Service
   Mrs. Fields, Inc.
   333 Main Street.
   Park City, Utah 84060